William Pitt the Younger

IN THE SAME SERIES

General Editors: Eric J. Evans and P. D. King

William Pitt the Younger

Eric J. Evans

London and New York

First published 1999
by Routledge
11 New Fetter Lane, London EC4P 4EE

Simultaneously published in the USA and Canada
by Routledge
29 West 35th Street, New York, NY 10001

©1999 Eric J. Evans

Typeset in Bembo by Routledge
Printed and bound in Great Britain by Clays Ltd, St Ives plc

British Library Cataloguing in Publication Data
A catalogue record for this book is available from the British Library

Library of Congress Cataloging in Publication Data
Evans, Eric J.,
William Pitt the Younger / Eric J. Evans.
p.   cm – (Lancaster pamphlets)
Includes bibliographical references (p.   ).
1. Pitt, William, 1759–1806. 2. Great Britain–Politics and
government–1760–1820. 3. Prime ministers–Great Britain–Biography.
I. Title. II. Series.
DA522.P6E93   1999
941.07'3'092–dc21   98–47724

ISBN 0–415–13285–1

Contents

Foreword

Lancaster Pamphlets offer concise and up-to-date accounts of major historical topics, primarily for the help of students preparing for Advanced Level examinations, though they should also be of value to those pursuing introductory courses in universities and other institutions of higher education. Without being all-embracing, their aims are to bring some of the central themes or problems confronting students and teachers into sharper focus than the textbook writer can hope to do; to provide the reader with some of the results of recent research which the textbook may not embody; and to stimulate thought about the whole interpretation of the topic under discussion.

Acknowledgements

I am extremely grateful to my co-editor, David King, and to Jen Carr for reading through the manuscript and for making their characteristically careful and helpful suggestions. I am also grateful to Heather McCallum for her patience in waiting for the delivery of this manuscript while a Series Editor wrestled with the problems of being Head of Department. All errors are, of course, my own responsibility.

Eric J. Evans
Lancaster
September 1998

Time Chart

1759   28 May: Pitt born at Hayes Place, south London, the second son
        of William Pitt the Elder and his wife Hester Grenville

1773   Attends Cambridge University but in residence there mostly
        from 1776–79

1780   December: Pitt elected MP for Appleby (Westmorland), aged 21
        years and 7 months; takes his seat in the Commons, January 1781

1782   July: Becomes Chancellor of the Exchequer in Shelburne's admin-
        istration, aged 23 years and 1 month; serves throughout Shelburne's
        prime ministership, resigning with him in February 1783

1783   September: Treaty of Versailles formally gives independence to
        the American colonies; 19 December: Pitt accepts George III's
        invitation to become Prime Minister, aged 24 years and 7 months;
        in the early months he has no majority in the Commons

1784   March: General election gives Pitt a comfortable majority over
        his main opponents, Charles James Fox and Lord North; his
        government now secure; Pitt's Commutation Act begins his
        financial and taxation reforms, greatly reducing duties on tea

1785   Pitt introduces parliamentary reform bill which is defeated in the
        Commons by 74 votes; no ministry introduces parliamentary
        reform again until Grey in March 1831; tax on shops introduced,
        but it fails to produce anticipated revenue; Pitt introduces
        proposals for mutually reduced tariffs between Britain and
        Ireland but the legislature of both countries reject them

1786   Pitt establishes sinking fund to reduce government debt; the
        Eden Trade Treaty signed between England and France

1787 'Free ports' agreement between Britain and United States begins to rebuild trading relationship between the two countries

1788 April: Alliance with Dutch ends Britain's diplomatic isolation in Europe; accession of Prussia in August creates the Triple Alliance; October: beginnings of King's illness (often thought to be porphyria) which rendered him incapable of discharging his duties; the Regency crisis threatens to end Pitt's ministry, since the Prince of Wales was anti-Pitt

1789 February: King's recovery ends the Regency crisis and secures Pitt's position; July: fall of the Bastille prison in Paris begins French Revolution

1790 First signs of division within Foxite Whig party with publication of Burke's *Reflections on the Revolution in France*; Burke and Fox publicly fall out

1791 Publication of Part I of Tom Paine's *Rights of Man* as counter-blast to Burke's book helps to develop radical consciousness in Britain; anti-reform activity – the Priestley Riots – in Birmingham; Pitt declares that Britain will be neutral in any European war launched against French revolutionaries

1792 Publication of Part II of *Rights of Man*; London Corresponding Society formed; radical Whigs form Society of the Friends of the People; Royal Proclamations against Seditious Writings indicate growing government concern about democratic movements in Britain

1793 February: First Coalition against France signed by Britain, Prussia, Holland, Spain and Austria; the coalition had fallen apart by 1795; Britain declares war on France

1794 May: government suspends Habeas Corpus Amendment Act as rising radical activity in Britain causes alarm; July: split within opposition Whig camp widened when Duke of Portland and other conservative Whigs join with Pitt in a pro-war and anti-reform coalition; Pitt's majority in the Commons and Lords now huge on most issues

1795 Beginnings of economic crisis and rising food prices stimulate radical and democratic organisations in many towns and cities; much support for a 'patriotic' and anti-reformist line also; June–October: unsuccessful support to counter-revolutionaries in France; war goes badly in most areas; Holland over-run and becomes 'Batavian Republic'; declares war on Britain; December: passage of the 'Two Acts': Treasonable Practices and Seditious

Meetings helps to reduce numbers supporting radical societies and to drive radicalism underground

1796 Peace talks between Britain and France fail; October: Spain enters war against Britain; December: attempted French invasion of Britain from Ireland fails

1797 Year of crisis in both the economy and the war; Pitt considers resignation; February: Bank of England suspends cash payments as British debt soars; French attempt to land in Fishguard (West Wales) as preliminary to invasion; April–May: naval mutinies at Spithead and the Nore; October: Admiral Duncan defeats Dutch fleet at Camperdown; Austrians sign Treaty of Campo Formio, leaving Britain isolated in war with French

1798 Pitt increases taxes, including taxes on newspapers in an effort to reduce reading of 'dangerous' literature by the lower orders; proposals for an income tax introduced; May: Napoleon's invasion of Egypt begins, reducing immediate invasion threat, although beginning of rebellion in Ireland seemed to offer fresh opportunities for a time; August: French fleet defeated by Napoleon at Aboukir Bay; December: alliance with Russia signed

1799 Income tax levied on British property owners for the first time; June: Second Coalition against France signed by Britain, Russia, Austria, Turkey, Portugal and Naples; this collapsed in 1801; radical organisations, The London Corresponding Society and the Society of United Irishmen, formally banned; Combinations Act makes all 'combinations in restraint of trade' (trades unions) illegal, though most were already outside the law anyway

1800 March: after much arm-twisting and some bribery, Act of Union between Britain and Ireland signed; September: Britain captures Malta; December: 'Armed Neutrality of the North' signed by Russia, Sweden, Denmark and Prussia in response to Britain's attempt to establish rights of search on all ships

1801 14 March: after disagreement with George III over Roman Catholic Emancipation, Pitt (aged 41 years and 9 months) resigned, to be replaced as Prime Minister by Addington; his first ministry had lasted for 17 years and almost 3 months; his resignation breaks up the 'Pittite coalition'; many of Pitt's ministers remain in government but others, importantly Grenville, refuse to support Addington and move closer to Fox; March–April: British fleet defeats Danes in reprisal for armed neutrality; October: discussions about peace with France begin

1802   March: Peace of Amiens ends the first phase of the French Wars; for the most part, conquests between Britain and France handed back; Pitt privately concerned at some of the terms but continues to support Addington publicly

1803   May: war resumes; pressure on Addington, largely from Fox-Grenville coalition; Pitt finds it increasingly difficult to maintain support for the ministry and is critical of Addington's financial policies

1804   January–April: Addington's ministry in ever greater trouble; King wishes Pitt to come back into office; Pitt attempts to produce a broader-based administration, bringing in supporters of Fox and Grenville. George vetoes any approach to Fox; 10 May: Addington resigns and Pitt resumes office as Prime Minister, aged 44 years and 11 months; December: Spain declares war on Britain

1805   Pitt, his parliamentary position never so strong in his second ministry as in his first, brings Addington (now Lord Sidmouth) back into government; April: Treaty of St Petersburg brings Russia into war against France; May: Dundas (now Lord Melville) forced to resign after allegations of financial and other irregularities while Treasurer of the Navy; his departure significantly weakens the government; July: Addington resigns; August: Austria's joins the Anglo-Russian alliance to form the Third Coalition against France; October: Napoleon defeats the Austrians at Ulm; Nelson decisively defeats a Franco-Spanish fleet off Cape Trafalgar; December: Napoleon's decisive victory over the Austrians at Austerlitz leads to peace between France and Austria and the collapse of the Third Coalition

1806   23 January: Pitt dies at Bowling Green House, Putney Heath (a house he rented), aged 46 years and 7 months; his second administration had lasted 1 year and 8 months; in all, the younger Pitt was Prime Minister for 18 years and 11 months, a senior minister of George III for 19 years and 8 months, and a Member of Parliament for 25 years and 1 month

1

The Making of a Prime Minister

Introduction: Pitt and the popular imagination

The Younger Pitt died almost two centuries ago. Inevitably, memories of a long-dead political leader – even one so eminent and important as Pitt – have faded from popular consciousness. Few, other than British historians, have much of an impression of him nowadays. Visitors to the National Portrait Gallery in London can absorb the flattering official portrait by John Hoppner. It shows a spare, controlled and upright figure in early middle age, possessed of fine features and a kindly gaze. This was not the image portrayed by contemporary cartoonists. Though they all represented a thinness unusual in prosperous politicians of the late eighteenth century, well used to lavish entertainment, large meals and fine wines, Pitt's kindly gaze was usually replaced by grave determination in portrayals by government supporters. His many opponents in the 1790s, hostile both to the government's persecution of reformers and to its taxation policies, represented him as cold, thin-lipped and almost manic in his rapacious intensity.

Every quiz buff will know that Pitt was the youngest Prime Minister in British history and will probably know that, unusually, he died in office. Some will be able to recall his last words (apparently well-enough authenticated): 'Oh, my country! How I leave my country' – a reference to its plight at the time of his death. Britain was locked in a long and bloody conflict with France which was still far from resolution. Indeed, the last confirmed report Pitt received of the war, just before his death in January 1806, was of Napoleon's crushing defeat of Britain's Austrian allies at

1

[handwritten note: 'Oh my country! How I leave my country.']

Austerlitz. A few might recall from old school lessons vague ideas about a Prime Minister allegedly 'good in peacetime but a poor war leader'. Those who have seen the 1942 film *The Young Mr Pitt*, directed by Carol Reed and starring Robert Donat as Pitt and Robert Morley as Charles James Fox, will retain the powerfully manipulated image of a noble patriot who sacrificed both domestic comforts (Pitt never married) and personal priorities (the restorer of the nation's finances is portrayed here as neglecting his own money needs) to provide selfless leadership to a nation in peril. It is as well to remember that this film was a piece of wartime propaganda. Audiences were expected to translate William Pitt's virtues in standing alone against the French in the 1790s into Winston Churchill's in doing much the same against the Germans in the 1940s. In truth, the implied comparison was far from exact. No one could deny either man's patriotism but the cynic might be inclined to suggest that the only other attribute the two war leaders had in common was one certainly not suggested by the film: they both drank extremely heavily.

Retained images of Pitt, however, take us little further. Some will have in their minds the physical and emotional contrast with his great political opponent Fox: the former lean, disciplined and good at figures, the latter fat, emotional and much better with people. This, too, only lightly scratches the surface of a much more complex, and multi-faceted, reality. What is clear is that William Pitt the Younger is well worth the effort to understand. He was Prime Minister for longer than anyone else, except his eminent predecessor Sir Robert Walpole. His period of office spanned perhaps the two most profoundly significant changes to have occurred in modern history – the French Revolution, which challenged (and eventually transformed) the political order of Europe, and the Industrial Revolution which began in Britain at much the same time and whose consequences eventually affected the lives of virtually every individual on the planet. Pitt was a leader of great gifts who, at the height of his powers, exercised a dominance over both parliament and his monarch which very few Prime Ministers have equalled. Though very few politicians remember it now, and he would certainly have disclaimed the title, Pitt also has a reasonable claim to be considered the first leader of the modern Conservative Party. Throughout his long tenure as Prime Minister, he was also his own Chancellor of the Exchequer. The priority implied by his dual office-holding is highly significant. No other Prime Minister (with the possible exception of Gladstone) has ever demonstrated such profound understanding of the nation's changing finances over a long period.

2

The well-cleared path to power

No major leader was so steeped in politics from his earliest years as the younger Pitt. He is, of course, 'Pitt the Younger' because of 'Pitt the Elder'. This Pitt, also a William, was Prime Minister when his second son was born on 28 May 1759, the greatest year of his prime ministership, since a string of impressive military and naval victories vindicated his bold strategy during the so-called Seven Years' War (1756–63). The Younger Pitt was the fourth of five children born between 1755 and 1761. His mother, Hester, whom the elder Pitt had married in 1754, was a Grenville, and thus a member of an even more established Whig political family. Her three brothers – Richard (from 1752 Earl Temple), George and James – all served in the Pitt-Newcastle government of 1757–61, though Temple and George Grenville later fell out with the elder Pitt. George was himself Prime Minister from 1763 to 1765. The Grenville-Pitt connection extended fruitfully into the next generation. George's own son, William Wyndham Grenville, would be a senior minister of the younger Pitt in the 1780s and 1790s, rising to be both Home Secretary and Foreign Secretary; he was also one of Pitt's most trusted confidants. William Grenville, indeed, was to succeed his cousin as Prime Minister, albeit briefly, in 1806.

William was educated at home (largely because of his father's detestation of the brutality of Eton, his own school) before going to Cambridge University in 1773. Here he had a number of false starts, largely due to illness, and went into normal residence only in 1776, leaving the university in 1779. Of Pitt's extraordinary intellectual gifts, there is no doubt. He absorbed the political implications of events almost as he absorbed infant milk. At the age of 7, when told of his father's ennoblement as Earl of Chatham, he reflected on his subordinate position in a now aristocratic family. He informed his tutor that 'he was glad he was not the eldest son, but that he could serve the country in the House of Commons like his papa' (Ehrman, I, 6). By 1772, Lady Chatham was writing to her husband: 'The fineness of William's mind makes him enjoy with the highest pleasure what would be above the reach of any other creature of his small age' (Stanhope, I, 4).

Pitt seems to have inherited looks, hard-headedness and financial acumen alike from his mother's side of the family. Regrettably for his family, he was to deploy these latter two attributes much more extensively on national than on personal affairs. His distinctive profile, the joy of so many cartoonists in the 1790s, bears a remarkable similarity to that of his mother in the portrait by Hudson. Lady Chatham spent most of the last years of her husband's life sorting out the consequences of his grandiosity and wastefulness. The elder Pitt, who had been living extravagantly beyond his means more or less consistently since leaving office in 1761, left debts of £20,000 on his death in 1778. Though these were written off by the state, the Chatham income proved insufficient either to allow his widow to maintain an aristocratic lifestyle or to provide the young William with sufficient income to cover his living expenses in Cambridge. From the late 1770s Pitt began raising loans to sustain the family. The taste for personal borrowing never left him. He raised almost £7,000 to buy a fine house and farm in Kent in 1785–6 – a sum which, as he acknowledged to his friend William Wilberforce, he could ill afford (Ehrman, I, 591). On his death in 1806, parliament responded much as it had done with his father. It voted a sum of £40,000 towards paying his personal debts. His tangled financial affairs were not finally sorted out for a further fifteen years (Ehrman, III, 834–5).

Early family talk that the bright second son would take up a legal career came to little. Pitt did reside in Lincoln's Inn for a time in 1780 but it was always clear that his passion was politics. An appetite that was whetted in infancy by close proximity to his father and uncles became ravenous after he attended the highly charged parliamentary debates of 1778–80 when Lord North's government was being lambasted by the opposition, particularly the Whig group led by the Marquess of Rockingham.

Pitt made an unsuccessful attempt on the parliamentary seat of Cambridge University in 1779 but his connections and abilities ensured that he did not have to wait long to enter parliament. A Cambridge friend, the Marquess of Granby, – who had recently succeeded to the Dukedom of Rutland – was politically linked to the great Cumbrian landowner and entrepreneur Sir James Lowther. Lowther – in the way of eighteenth-century politics – had direct control of a number of parliamentary boroughs. He put one of them, Appleby in Westmorland, at the disposal of the younger Pitt, all expenses paid. The few electors of that pleasant market town were only very rarely put to the trouble of an election. No contest had been held there since 1754; none would be held until the Great Reform Act of 1832 which erased the borough from the electoral map. The younger Pitt was nominated in November 1780, was 'elected' the following month and took his seat in the Commons in January 1781. He was just short of 22 years old. Though such rapid progress would be highly unusual in the twentieth century, it was common enough in the eighteenth. 'Rotten' or 'managed' boroughs were a recognised route for able, well-connected politicians of tender age to reach parliament. It gave them plenty of time to absorb the atmosphere, learn their trade and then, in time, exercise political leadership.

What *was* unusual about Pitt, however, was the speed of his progress once in parliament. Within twenty months, he was Chancellor of the Exchequer; within thirty-five, Prime Minister. Such a precipitous upward trajectory requires explanation. It comes through a combination of two remarkable factors: Pitt's own abilities and the destruction of political stability at the end of the disastrous war fought by Britain in a vain attempt to stop the colonies of America's eastern seaboard from claiming their independence.

Pitt's early parliamentary speeches made an immediate impact. His first, on 26 February 1781, was generously applauded both by the Prime Minister, Lord North, and by North's most eloquent critic, Charles James Fox. Burke is said to have remarked that, as Chatham's son, 'He was not a chip of [sic] the old block; he is the old block itself' (Ehrman, I, 52). What impressed, apart from the delivery and an already well-honed attentiveness to the mood of the House, was the precocious authority and mastery of subject matter. Calm, informed authority at a time of mounting political crisis was a prime asset. He spoke relatively rarely, making about twenty speeches between January 1781 and July 1782, but always with effect. Henry Dundas, a shrewd and experienced observer, praised his 'first-rate abilities…and…most persuasive eloquence' (Ehrman, I, 55).

Another necessary attribute was Pitt's stance as a reformer in the early part of his career. Reform had moved steadily up the political agenda during the prime ministership of Lord North (1770–82) and its significance for Pitt's career is explored in more detail in Chapter 2. Here it need only be stated that demands for parliamentary and administrative reform were a prime weapon in the mounting anti-government campaign from 1778 onwards. By early 1781, when Pitt arrived in parliament, it was clear that Lord North's administration, which had to that point been by far the most stable of George III's reign, was in serious trouble. Its parliamentary majorities were dwindling steadily and on some high-profile issues during 1780 it had actually been defeated. Opposition groups eagerly exploited both reverses in America and the government's apparent inability to handle demands from Protestants in Ireland for greater self-government.

North's government was undermined by its failure to control discontent and rebellion in its two most important colonies. News of the decisive surrender of British troops at Yorktown in October 1781 caused North to remark 'Oh God, it is all over'. In fact, it was not – quite. The King kept him uncomfortably and embarrassedly in office for a further six months while the authority of Britain's government dwindled almost to nothing. North's eventual resignation in March 1782 began one of the most turbulent two years in British parliamentary history. From it, the younger Pitt emerged, against all expectation, as the decisive victor.

Pitt inevitably ranged himself with the opposition to North, echoing his father's position in the 1770s that the Prime Minister's American policy was misconceived and disastrous. He also spoke about the increasingly fractious relations between King and parliament. North's ministry was replaced in March 1782 by a coalition of anti-North Whigs under the Marquess of Rockingham, leader of the largest and most effective group of Whig reformers. It contained, as Home and Foreign Secretaries respectively, the Earl of Shelburne and Charles James Fox. Though it seems strange to modern eyes, Pitt (at 22 years of age and with fourteen months' parliamentary experience) was seriously considered for a ministerial post. His status as Chatham's son carried substantial weight and he was close to Shelburne, who had himself come to prominence as one of the ablest of Chatham's supporters. Furthermore, the initial impression he had made was, as we have seen, extremely favourable. Pitt certainly had the supreme self-confidence to announce to the Commons in March 1782: 'For myself, I could not expect to form part of a new administration; but were my doing so more within my reach, I feel myself bound to declare that I would never accept a subordinate situation' (Stanhope, I, 70).

Perhaps he already foresaw that the new ministry, which George III thoroughly disliked, and which was internally divided particularly by the rivalry and mutual dislike of Shelburne and Fox, was unlikely to last long and that his own reputation would not be enhanced by association with it. In fact, it was brought to a premature close by Rockingham's sudden death at the beginning of July. Shelburne had already been angling with the King for a realignment of ministers which would see Fox downgraded, if not replaced. The King speedily announced that Shelburne would be his new Prime Minister, whereupon Fox (and most of the old Rockinghams) resigned. The Shelburne ministry was, therefore, significantly different in composition from the Rockingham one and Shelburne had need of new talent to replace the experienced, if antagonistic, ministers who went out with, or soon after, Fox. Pitt was an obvious choice and could hardly describe the Chancellorship of the Exchequer (though the office had less prestige then than now) as a 'subordinate situation'.

Pitt served throughout Shelburne's ministry, which lasted from July 1782 to February 1783. Its work was dominated by proposals for peace with the victorious American colonies and Pitt was duly supportive of the efforts made. It was also concerned with administrative reform and here Pitt took a more prominent line, carrying forward Shelburne's plans for customs reform and for tighter controls on public offices. The bills passed the Commons before being rejected in the Lords and they are important as an early indication of two of Pitt's great passions: saving government money by efficient deployment of resources, and attempting to ensure that remuneration of offices should be on the basis of public service and not political advantage.

Shelburne's ministry was brought down by parliamentary arithmetic. Fox, now clearly in charge of the Rockingham group of reformist Whigs (although he formally deferred to the Duke of Portland), had been scheming to bring his rival down. He calculated that, with the support of North's followers, he could deprive Shelburne of a parliamentary majority and force his resignation. He was right. By early 1783, with the American issue virtually settled, Fox and North had far less to disagree about than previously. North's political ambition continued to burn bright and his easy charm made him a useful leader of a substantial parliamentary group. The two men reached an agreement early in February and tested it out in two motions criticising Shelburne's government in the middle of the month. On 24 February, Shelburne resigned.

This outcome outraged the King on at least three grounds. First, he was by no means convinced that Shelburne had to go; in his view, the Prime Minister could have fought on to test the durability of this new grouping. Second, he hated Fox and most of his supporters with a passion. Third, he had reposed absolute faith in North as his Prime Minister for almost twelve years. A combination of interests between Foxites and Northites he thought of as virtual treason. It was, to him, proof of the view he had held when he came to the throne in 1760: that established politicians were motivated by greed and personal ambition, rather than by any desire to provide good government. For five weeks, while Britain tottered on virtually without any government, he tried to hold back the logic of a Fox-North administration – that 'infamous coalition' as he was to call it. Significantly, he turned first to Pitt to rescue him from his difficulty. Pitt at first agreed to become Prime Minister before having second thoughts, based on the calculation that North would probably continue to oppose and that his own position, therefore, could be made no stronger than Shelburne's had latterly been.

Pitt's decision probably reflected a deeper calculation, too. He knew well enough how outraged the King was by the prospect of a government led by Fox and North. If the King found no other first minister in the meantime, he would accept it with an exceedingly ill grace and would work to ensure that it had as difficult, and as short, a lease on power as possible. Pitt would prefer to come into office after a discredited government had failed, rather than before a numerically powerful coalition had been tried. Perhaps this is to invest Pitt with too much prescience. However, contemporaries were impressed with him. The Duke of Grafton recorded in his diary:

The good judgment of so young a man, who, not void of ambition on this trying occasion, could refuse this splendid offer, adds much to the lustre of the character he had acquired, for it was a temptation sufficient to have offset the resolution of most men.

(Stanhope, I, 109–10)

The details of the Fox-North coalition (nominally headed by the Duke of Portland) need not concern us. It concluded peace with the American colonies and it did command majorities in the House of Commons. However, it never had the remotest chance of winning over the King, who, as Pitt had assumed, schemed against it from the beginning. In December 1783 he exerted massive influence on the House of Lords to persuade it to reject the coalition's important bill for the government of India. This defeat he then chose to interpret (on scant warrant) as a public loss of confidence in the Fox-North administration, which he proceeded summarily to dismiss. There is evidence that Pitt gave unofficial advice to the King on how the dismissal of his hated ministry might be effected. As in February, his first choice of replacement was Pitt, and this time Pitt did not turn him down.

Why was Pitt the King's choice to resolve the most substantial political crisis of his reign? We can take it as read both that the King appreciated Pitt's gifts and that he recognised also that in his brief parliamentary career he had created a universally strong impression. By December 1783, he was disposed to believe that if any minister could extricate him from the constitutional difficulties in which he found himself, that minister was William Pitt. But there was much more to it than this. Both the family name, and its political reputation, mattered. George had not always seen eye to eye with the Earl of Chatham, especially when the latter was in office, but Chatham did not come from that hated group of Whig politicians which had been collectively known as the 'Old Corps'. These politicians George III accused of using unconstitutional stratagems to reduce the powers of monarchy almost to nothing. He considered the Rockingham group to be their malign successors, intent now on depriving the monarch of the most precious power of all: his right to choose his own ministers. Pitt was never a royal toady; indeed, he shared some of the Rockingham concerns about royal influence, though to a milder degree. He did, however, both recognise and respect the constitutional position of the sovereign and he was not inclined either to bluster or to dictate to George. He respected the convention that he was genuinely taking office as 'the King's minister', with all that the phrase implied for royal choice. The irony was that, as we shall see (Chapter 5),

Pitt's own reforms would do more long-term damage to the independent powers of the monarchy than any of the direct constitutional confrontations of the early 1780s. On 19 December 1783, he took office as Prime Minister and First Lord of the Treasury.

2

Pitt the Political Reformer

Reform in Opposition

In view of Pitt's later reputation as the scourge of parliamentary reformers (Chapter 7), it is important to stress his own early support for parliamentary reform. Like almost all opposition politicians in the late 1770s and early 1780s, he believed that an important cause of the nation's difficulties was that the political system had become resistant to reform and that the King and his courtiers had assumed excessive power. The independence of parliament, in the reformers' judgement, was threatened by the excessive influence wielded there by George III and his political managers, who placed compliant supporters in office for no better reason than that they voted reliably the right way.

This viewpoint was elegantly encapsulated in the parliamentary motion presented by the Chathamite MP John Dunning in April 1780: 'that the influence of the crown has increased, is increasing and ought to be diminished'. Less well known, but equally important as indicating what reformers wished to do about the situation, is the next clause. This claimed parliamentary scrutiny of court revenues as a check on royal power:

> That it is competent to this House to examine into, and to correct, abuses in the expenditure of the civil list revenues [i.e. revenues voted by parliament but controlled directly by the crown], as well as in every other branch of the public revenue, whenever it shall appear expedient to the wisdom of this House to do so.

> (O'Gorman, 1975, 418)

One very important reason why the North government faltered so badly in its later years was that opposition politicians convinced the large numbers of MPs who acknowledged no party political loyalties, of the need for reform. Support from these 'independents' was crucial to the stability of government. By 1781, partly because of the activities of opposition politicians and partly because of the growth and vitality of extra-parliamentary organisations such as Christopher Wyvill's 'County Association Movement' and the 'Westminster Association', North's government could no longer count on such support.

Almost all Pitt's early parliamentary speeches concerned reform in one form or another. In May 1782, two months before coming into office under Shelburne, he proposed a motion to investigate the prospects for parliamentary reform. His speech reflected widespread contemporary concerns: 'the people were loud for a *more equal representation,* as one of the most likely means to protect their country from danger, and themselves from oppressive taxes' (Ehrman, I, 70). This sentiment would not have been out of place in the mouth of a Chartist democrat on a public platform in the late 1830s or early 1840s. Other parts of the speech, however, stressed the Chathamite legacy: concern for 'moderation' and a determination to dislodge the unsightly barnacles attached to 'a beautiful form of government' rather than any attempt to create a new one based on 'vague and chimerical speculations'. His motion was lost by only twenty votes.

Pitt's second attempt to secure parliamentary reform took place exactly one year later. Again, he tried to calm the more conservative spirits in the Commons: 'His object at present was not to innovate but rather to renew and invigorate the spirit of the constitution, without deviating materially from its present form'. Now, however, he presented specific proposals: to outlaw bribery at elections; to disfranchise manifestly corrupt parliamentary boroughs; to create a significant number of additional MPs for the counties and larger boroughs (Evans, 1996, 398). To the Yorkshire reformer Christopher Wyvill, he had talked two months earlier of creating at least 100 new county members. The thinking here was that county MPs were elected by larger numbers of voters than were most borough members; their reputation for independence of thought and action was also greater. Pitt was not confident enough to make such a radical proposal and he also assured members that he had no desire to increase the number of voters, thinking this 'subversive of liberty' (Ehrman, I, 75). The proposal, however, was decisively defeated – by 293 votes to 149. North's supporters in the new Fox-North coalition voted almost to a man against it. Those backing Pitt included supporters of Fox, the remaining Chathamites and, significantly, almost half the county MPs,

11

together with a fair smattering of members elected for the first time (like Pitt himself) in 1780. Pitt was probably justified in considering that the mere passage of time would produce a better outcome in a year or two.

All governments during the crisis of 1782–4 were reformist in some manner but the reformers in parliament were far from united. Some were much more concerned with what was called 'economical reform' – cutting out royal influence, reducing the number of crown appointees, and the like; others were primarily parliamentary reformers. Among parliamentary reformers, it was far easier to obtain agreement on broad principles than on specific details. There were also the inevitable personality clashes and rivalries born of ambition. As early as 1782, a clear breach had opened up between Pitt and Shelburne on the one hand and the Foxites on the other. Reform, it seemed by December 1783, was a necessary recommendation for a minister (whatever George III might prefer) but it was by no means a sufficient condition for successful government.

The general election of 1784

Fox believed that his dismissal by George III would backfire. His calculation was that the manoeuvres which led up to it publicly revealed the King's deviousness and unconstitutional scheming. He expected that his own brand of reform would now prove more palatable to public opinion than that of Mr Pitt. Fox believed that it would be easy to present the new Prime Minister as the puppet of an over-mighty monarch. Furthermore, Fox and his allies still held a substantial parliamentary majority. The wife of the Rockingham Whig John Crewe quickly dubbed Pitt's new ministry 'the mince-pie' administration, since it was unlikely to see out the Christmas season (Mitchell, 1992, 67). The list of Pitt's ministers did not inspire confidence either; it looked especially weak in the lower House. Those later great mainstays of Pitt's governments, Henry Dundas and his cousin William Grenville, were still inexperienced and held only minor office. Meanwhile, heavyweights such as Shelburne, John Robinson and the King's trusted adviser and 'fixer' Charles Jenkinson were excluded.

Unfortunately for Fox, what he saw as weaknesses, Pitt rapidly turned to strengths. The absence of Shelburne strongly implied that Pitt meant to be his own man, while the exclusion of Jenkinson neatly made the point to independent MPs that the new Prime Minister was no royal cipher. Pitt's strategy in the early months of 1784 was to demonstrate capability and authority in parliament, despite the substantial majorities theoretically arrayed against him. After the Commons reassembled in January, Pitt suffered two defeats to Foxite majorities of 39 and 54 (Mitchell, 1992, 68) but continued to govern undaunted. His authority in the face of adversity was certainly impressive but it is likely that Fox's fundamental political miscalculations mattered more. Though the King was certainly averse to having Fox back in government, Pitt was more equivocal. Learning that many independents were touting a Fox-Pitt coalition as the best solution to the continuing crisis, he put out one or two tentative olive branches to Fox. The two men's political enmity, after all, was very recent and still had shallow roots. Both acknowledged themselves to be reformers. A Fox-Pitt coalition in February 1784 would have seemed much less strange than the Fox-North coalition which had been contrived ten months earlier.

Perhaps to Pitt's relief, however, Fox was not receptive. He saw no reason why he should serve under the younger and far less experienced Pitt. He also had his huge constitutional fish to fry. He was determined to present his dismissal as proof of the King's contempt both for the Commons and for public opinion. His stance came close to denying George's right to choose his own ministers. Such a blatant constitutional confrontation was more than many even of his own supporters could stomach. Most of North's supporters (though significantly not North himself) swung over to Pitt's side. Outside Westminster, many parliamentary reformers – faced with an unwelcome choice between reformist heavyweights in the Commons – also expressed a preference for Pitt's moderation over what they considered Fox's extremism. In truth, Charles James Fox was playing on a one-string fiddle and, not for the last time in a chequered political career, his lack of perspective told against him. Majorities for Fox dwindled rapidly during late January and February 1784 and when, on 8 March, a motion which included the call for Pitt's dismissal was passed in the Commons by a single vote, it was clear that the tide was flowing uncontrollably against him. Pitt, who had delayed asking the King to dissolve parliament and call a general election while he consolidated his own position and reputation, both in parliament and in the country, now asked for a dissolution. George eagerly agreed; parliament was dissolved on 25 March 1784.

Conspiracy theorists, common enough among Fox's increasingly beleaguered supporters, could see this initiative as further evidence of the King's evil design. They did not dispute the King's *right* to dissolve parliament. They were, however, well aware that, since the Septennial Act of 1716 had extended the life of parliament to a maximum of seven years, premature dissolutions had been exceedingly rare. The convention had been for parliaments to run almost to their maximum permitted length. Only one since 1715 had lasted less than five and a half years, and that had been because the death of George I in 1727 had automatically necessitated a general election. By contrast, the parliament which assembled in October 1780 lasted only three and a half years. It was dissolved early for one purpose only: so that Pitt, the King's favoured minister, would be given maximum opportunity to gain a parliamentary majority at the expense of Fox.

The plan worked. What were quickly dubbed 'Fox's Martyrs' went down to electoral defeat in droves; roughly 160 lost their seats. There is no doubt that the King exerted maximum effort in constituencies where he had influence to ensure their defeat, but the election was also won for Pitt in constituencies where it was almost impossible to bribe one's way to victory. Pitt had significant victories in the larger boroughs and, perhaps more unexpectedly, in many of the county seats – not least the highly populated ones of Middlesex and Yorkshire. Fox himself was run desperately close in Westminster, where he was opposed by some prominent reformers. Such an outcome would not have been possible unless Pitt had been able to present himself both as a reformer and as a supporter of 'clean' government. Fox's lurid misrepresentation that Pitt was a pawn in the hands of an unconstitutional monarch was widely, even contemptuously, rejected by public opinion. Some historians have even characterised the 1784 election in terms of an emerging sense of 'Englishness': 'A vote against Fox was a vote for the National Identity and National Independence, and a vote for Pitt was the elector's affirmation of his own morality and identity as a true Englishman' (Newman, 1997, 218). This judgement is dubious – not least because Fox's attacks on monarchical power had a distinctly patriotic tinge – and also pretentious, but 1784 was a watershed just the same.

The size, and humiliation, of Fox's defeat served to distort his political judgement still further. Pitt was now almost as much hated as the King while Fox's overwhelming objective was to destroy the political influence of George III. It was a fatally flawed strategy which unfolding events would only serve to make still more unrealistic. It did much to ensure that Pitt would remain Prime Minister for almost seventeen years: some 'mince-pie'!

The parliamentary reform proposals of 1785

Pitt did not renege on his credentials as a parliamentary reformer. He told Rev. Christopher Wyvill in March 1784 that 'my zeal for Reform in Parliament is by no means abated' and then in December he would 'exert his whole power *as a man, and as a minister and boldly,* to carry such a melio-

→ less intense.

14

rated system of representation as may place the constitution on a footing of permanent security' (Holland Rose, 1911, 197). In January 1785 he told his close friend the Duke of Rutland 'I really think that I see more than ever the chance of effecting a safe and temperate plan' (Ehrman, I, 225). He knew, of course, that the obstacles were formidable. The King did not like parliamentary reform, though Pitt extracted a promise from him not to oppose it openly. Many in his own government were luke-warm at best. In the Commons, those representing the smaller boroughs feared that they would lose their seats. Even among the reformers, many divisions surfaced. As with proportional representation in our own day, it was much easier to agree upon the general principle than to gain consensus for any specific scheme. Both inside and outside parliament, the reformers were split and these splits led to mutual distrust, particularly between Wyvill's 'county' supporters and the London reformers.

Pitt's own scheme was, by parliamentary standards, a radical one. It proposed to persuade the thirty-six smallest boroughs to give up their independent representation by offering their owners monetary compen-sation. Those seats which thus became available (a maximum of 72) would be transferred to the counties and to London. This would substantially increase the representativeness of the lower House. Pitt also proposed to increase the electorate in the counties by allowing copyholders and some leaseholders (as well as existing freeholders) to vote. It was estimated that this would increase the British electorate by about 30 per cent.

Despite Pitt's early optimism, his bill never had much chance of success. Pitt could not afford to make such a controversial measure an issue of confidence in his administration. Without this, his own supporters (including Grenville, among other ministers) did not feel any pressing need to vote for it. The support he got was piecemeal. Fox and the Rockinghams gave it grudging approval, while criticising the details. In addition to some personal support, almost thirty county representatives voted for it; this was a smaller number than had supported his earlier reform bill in 1783. He could also claim a clear majority among members who had been elected for the first time in 1784, which provided further evidence of the reformist temper of the voters at an election which Fox had condemned as rigged by court influence. None of this was remotely enough. Pitt went down to defeat by 248 votes to 174. Though the issue did not disappear – and Pitt himself was to become one of its most powerful opponents in the 1790s – this was as near as anyone would get for almost half a century. Few of the parliamentary reformers of 1785 would be alive to see the next Prime Minister to take up the issue, Earl Grey, achieve success in the very different world of 1832. Pitt was not tempted to take it up again, to the chagrin of his extra-parliamentary supporters. Ultimately, he was persuaded that other reforms, especially in administration and finance, had higher priority and on these he had no intention of being defeated.

3

Pitt and the 'National Revival', 1783–93

Financial and administrative reforms

The crisis which Pitt inherited on coming into office was as much economic as political. The value of national industrial and commercial production in real terms, which had been increasing substantially during the eighteenth century, fell during the 1770s. Exports declined by about 12 per cent during the same decade. In the years 1775–84, meanwhile, the size of the national debt increased by 91 per cent. In the first months of Pitt's government it stood at what all observers considered the perilously high level of £242.9 million (Holmes and Szechi, 1993, 368, 382, 388). The situation seemed out of control; during 1783 it has been estimated that the British state ran up a deficit of almost £11 million on an annual income of £23.5 million. The value of government stocks went down by more than 17 per cent during 1783, accurately reflecting declining confidence. William Grenville reflected later that in 1783–4 'the nation gave way…to an almost universal panic on the subject' (Ehrman, I, 158). The reason for all the turbulence, of course, was the American war which had only just ended when Pitt came to power.

The main thrust of Pitt's financial policy was, therefore, dictated for him. It was necessary to cut expenditure drastically while also raising new taxes to make good the shortfall. Pitt did both, but his temperament inclined him to place substantial stress on a third remedy: making sure that income theoretically due actually reached the exchequer by promoting efficiencies in collection. This lay at the heart of perhaps his most famous financial policy, which concerned smuggling. Smuggling was at least as important to the 'black economy' of the 1780s as illicit drug dealing became to that of the 1990s. It deprived the exchequer of huge amounts of revenue. In the nature of things we cannot be sure, but it is perfectly possible that as much as one-fifth of all imports came into the country illegally – a fair proportion of it into the rocky coves and sheltered inlets of the Cornish coast. Pitt's response was massively to reduce levels of taxation on the main goods which attracted the attention of smugglers. This made an illegal, and therefore risky, trade much less profitable. The tea trade was his main target. The import duty on tea was reduced from 119 per cent to a uniform 25 per cent by a 'Commutation Act' in 1784 (Evans, 1996, 26). At the same time revenue collection was substantially simplified. In 1784, also, Pitt amended the so-called 'Hovering Act' of 1780; officials could now search ships up to four leagues (approximately twelve miles) out to sea, rather than two leagues, as before. The incentives to smuggle were, therefore, further reduced by increased risks of detection. In 1785–7 duties on rum, wine, and brandy were reduced; increased legitimate consumption, however, ensured higher revenues despite reductions in duty rates. Food and raw material imports rose from approximately £13 million to £27 million between the mid-1780s and the mid-1790s.

Pitt had both a tactical and a strategic purpose in his taxation policies. Tactically, he fished around for new items to tax in order to reduce the government deficit. Strategically, he was concerned (as his great predecessor Sir Robert Walpole had been) to ensure that the main burden of taxes fell on property owners rather than the lower orders. Especially in peacetime, Hanoverian governments raised most of their revenue by indirect taxation (*i.e.* placing levies on goods which were consumed rather than on income). It was important, therefore, to lay the heaviest indirect taxes on goods disproportionately consumed by the well-off.

This was only partly altruistic. Successive Hanoverian governments knew that they could expect substantial popular discontent and even riot when prices of basic necessities – such as bread – shot up unexpectedly. Hence Pitt's apparently quirky preference for new taxes on horses used for pleasure, on hackney 'carriages, on hair-powder, on fashionable men's hats and on women's ribbons. The poor could not afford equestrian transport, were not conveyed in carriages, did not wear wigs and could not afford to follow fashion. Pitt also modified the window tax by introducing a new scale with larger properties paying substantially more. Predictably, property owners responded by sacrificing a little light to a heavy tax; they bricked up many of their windows. Humble items were not ignored altogether. Pitt levied a tax of a halfpenny (0.2p) a pound on candles, which

18

requiring the Treasury to give priority to the Fund when making payments. Pitt also increased taxes with the aim of ensuring that a government surplus of £1 million could be paid out each year for reduction of the National Debt. It was essential to Pitt's plan that surpluses be built up by taxation rather than by borrowing. Crucially, also, the Act placed administration of the fund in the hands of specially appointed 'Commissioners for Reducing the National Debt' to ensure optimum efficiency.

For several years, the scheme worked well. From 1786–93, the new commissioners received £8 million and invested it, reducing the debt by more than £10 million. The specific sums received were relatively modest; their main importance was psychological. A government committed to the achievement of regular surpluses inspired confidence in public finances and thereby helped to stimulate a climate of investment. This in turn helped the massive expansion of overseas trade during this period (see Chapter 4). In theory, the ultimate goal of Price's bright scheme – extinguishing the entire National Debt – might have been achievable. The arrival of yet another war in 1793 (see Chapter 6), and one of unprecedented cost, however, destroyed the rationale of the Sinking Fund. By the mid-1790s government debts were mounting alarmingly yet again. The National Debt rose from £243 million to £359 million in the years 1793–7 (Ehrman, III, 100). In this situation, the continued requirement to transfer upwards of £4 million a year into the Fund became a liability, although it was not widely recognised as such at the time. Pitt continued to believe until his death that it represented sound patriotic financial policy, which continued to give investors confidence. Only gingerly, and slowly, was the Fund abandoned by the Liverpool government in the 1820s.

Pitt's administrative policies aimed at cutting out waste. Though not specially ordered in his own business arrangements (he allowed correspondence to go unanswered for months – sometimes longer), he was always anxious to promote those who could help him run the governmental and administrative machine with maximum efficiency and minimum cost. This objective was, however, politically sensitive. The structure of politics depended on the system of patronage. Most government offices were filled, not on merit as demonstrated by competitive interview or examination, but by nomination from a person of influence. In late eighteenth-century Britain such a person would normally be either a member of the royal court or be nominated by an aristocratic patron.

In the late 1770s and early 1780s, the Rockingham Whigs had tried to reduce the number of patronage appointments, largely as a means of striking at royal influence. Pitt was realistic enough to know that any

21

direct assault on patronage would weaken his own position – not least with the King, who had, since his accession in 1760, used his powers of appointment as an effective means of bolstering his own position against opposition politicians. Pitt could not afford mass sackings of men who had little work to do but who were well connected. He kept Horace Walpole in the largely titular post of usher of Exchequer receipts until the old man's death in 1797 (Steven Watson, 1960, 284). Instead, Pitt moved cautiously – promoting men of proven capability, like Richard Frewin at Customs, and ensuring that, within the overall system, as much as possible was done to effect rationalisation and, where possible, economy. There were certainly some casualties. Lords Mountstuart and Sondes of the Treasury found themselves dismissed in 1785 after Pitt introduced a new statutory commission for auditing public accounts, although they received the enormous sum of £7,000 a year each as compensation. His initiative gave the Treasury greater control over what had become a famously complex procedure, affording plenty of opportunity for unscrupulous officials to line their own pockets. The new system was estimated to cost only a third as much as the old. The Board of Taxes and the Excise Board were also strengthened; financial administration and accountability were substantially tightened. Pitt's Consolidated Fund Act of 1787 also greatly simplified collection procedures and did away with most of the 103 separate Exchequer revenue accounts (Christie, 1982, 187).

Other important initiatives included replacing the old system of payment of fees with salaries for new appointments. The change implied a rate for the job rather than remuneration which might not relate at all to the nature of the task. The work of government employees was subjected to much greater inspection. In modern parlance, their productivity went up substantially. Important improvements to both army and naval administration were introduced, not least by Sir Charles Middleton (later Lord Barham), Comptroller of the Navy Office.

Pitt could not claim novelty for many of these administrative changes; several had been projected by North, Shelburne or the Fox–North coalition. Pitt, however, took them on, refined them and monitored their progress closely. British government was substantially more efficient and professional at the end of Pitt's prime ministership than it had been at the beginning. One important long-term political consequence of his determination to increase efficiency was that the patronage system began to wither. However inadvertently, Pitt's reforms prepared the way for the introduction of a fully professional civil service from the middle of the nineteenth century under the prompting of another reforming Prime Minister, William Gladstone.

Assessment

How much credit should Pitt claim for the so-called 'National Revival'? The historian who invented this phrase as part of the title of the first part of his biography was in no doubt. Pitt inherited a mess, and straightened it out. 'The war which ended in 1783 had been carried on in a singularly wasteful manner.' 'The difficulties' which he faced in reconstructing the nation's finances 'were enormous' and if it 'matured slowly', Pitt's 'financial genius' is nevertheless beyond dispute (Holland Rose, 1911, 179, 186, 187).

Historians in the second half of the twentieth century have been less inclined to hero worship. It is important to put the contribution of any individual – however able and dedicated, and the younger Pitt was both – into a wider context. There is much about a nation's economic performance which cannot be commanded by the policies of its governments. Britain's economic growth, based in substantial measure on the massive increase of overseas trade during the eighteenth century, had been only temporarily checked by the American war. With the return of peace, trade – not least with the newly independent United States – boomed once more. The value of British exports almost doubled overall between the mid-1780s and the mid-1790s, while those to the US increased by 125 per cent (Evans, 1996, 417). In the early stages of Britain's industrial revolution, moreover, manufactured goods contributed more than 80 per cent of the value of exports. Concern about the state of the nation in 1783 was rapidly seen to be alarmist. Pitt's inheritance was far less sickly than it appeared at the end of 1783.

Also, he inherited, and adapted, the ideas and policies of others. His indebtedness to Price over the Sinking Fund has already been noted. The partial rehabilitation of Lord North's reputation in recent years has also encompassed the recognition that his financial policies had important innovative features, some of which were developed by Pitt in the 1780s. Pitt's most distinguished biographer concedes that

> He [Pitt] was conservative in taxation – in some ways, perhaps, more conservative than North...when it came to the point it was usually North who had been there before him, and formed or adopted conclusions that most nearly resembled his own.
>
> (Ehrman, I, 277)

Pitt also learned much about finance from Shelburne.

Any balanced assessment must take account both of the basic strength of the British economy in the 1780s and of Pitt's indebtedness to others. This still leaves substantial scope for recognising Pitt's own merits.

Throughout his peacetime administrations, he showed remarkable sure-footedness. He directed taxation policy and debt reduction with skill and tenacity while his contribution to the reform of the governmental machine was massive. As Ehrman has pointed out, he achieved so much because he combined vision with practicality. He was able to yoke a 'strong instinct for perfection to his equally strong instinct for the possible' (Ehrman, I, 323).

4

Foreign and Commercial Policy, 1783–91

[handwritten: loss of America = GBR no allies]

In search of allies

The loss of the American colonies in 1783 was widely interpreted as a commercial disaster. It also left Britain isolated in European diplomacy. For most of the eighteenth century, Britain had been locked into an intricate complex of alliances. During the American war it seemed friendless in a Europe which was beginning to resent the country's commercial expansion and which regarded the outcome of the American conflict as a well-merited come-uppance. By the end of that conflict, Britain was at war with the three great powers of western Europe: France, Spain and the United Provinces (Holland), all of whom had joined the conflict in support of the American colonists.

Much the most important – and long-lasting – enmity was that with France. Since William III's wars with Louis XIV in the 1690s, France had been firmly installed as the national enemy. When Britain was not actually at war with France in the eighteenth century (as it was from 1702–13, 1740–8, 1756–63 and 1778–83), it had two overriding objectives: to ensure it prevented the French Bourbon monarchy from exerting diplomatic supremacy on the continent of Europe, and to sustain commercial supremacy in the Americas and in India. The second of these seemed to have been achieved by the end of the Seven Years' War but the outcome of the struggle in the Americas seemed to throw everything into doubt. In 1783, many European diplomats believed, in Professor Christie's words, that Britain was 'finished' (Christie, 1982, 193). The country, after all, had

25

had little clout in Europe for most of the time between the middle of the fifteenth century and the early eighteenth. Its renaissance during the end of the War of the Spanish Succession (and confirmed by the Treaty of Utrecht in 1713) had been as sudden as it had been surprising and it was perhaps understandable from the perspective of the courts of Paris, Vienna or Madrid to consider that the natural diplomatic order had been reasserted in 1783 with Britain returning to a peripheral role. France's ability to secure a defensive alliance with the United Provinces in 1785 only seemed to strengthen its hand.

The general, but by no means universal, assumption in Britain was that new alliances were urgently needed. As the MP and diplomat Sir James Harris wrote to the British Ambassador in Vienna soon after the Pitt ministry was formed 'To recover our weight on the continent by judicious alliances is the general wish of every man the least acquainted with the interests of this country' (Black, 1994, 13). He made this statement in support of the view that there was no reason to expect significant differences in an administration headed by Pitt from one headed by Fox or North. On the other hand, the King (whose influence in foreign affairs historians have until quite recently underplayed) was not convinced that close European alliances in order to counter France's ambitions were an advantage. He preferred to avoid commitments which risked dragging Britain into yet another war.

Pitt's foreign secretary, the Marquess of Carmarthen, had little initial success with a plan to rehabilitate Britain in European affairs by, as he put it to Pitt, 'separating…that unnatural alliance:…the House of Austria from France' (Black, 1991, 225) and making overtures to Joseph II, the Austrian Emperor. The complication here was George III. Hanoverian monarchs took a keen interest in British foreign affairs; they were, after all, Electors of Hanover and Hanover was a substantial state in northern Germany. In 1785, acting as Elector, George joined the anti-Austrian *Fürstenbund* (League of Princes) organised by Frederick the Great of Prussia. That was enough to kill Carmarthen's strategy.

As so often in eighteenth-century European diplomacy, however, the situation changed quickly. First, Frederick the Great died in 1786. Frederick, a close ally of Pitt's father during the Seven Years' War, had felt betrayed by Britain in the last years of that war after Pitt had left office. There was reason to suppose that his inexperienced successor, Frederick William II, might prove more amenable to diplomatic overtures from Britain once it was clear that neither country would be able to strike an alliance with Austria. The initial problem, however, was that the new King's advisers were pro-French.

Second, events in the United Provinces took a turn from which Britain could benefit. The political situation there was confused. Two groups vied for supremacy: the 'Orangists', supporters of the hereditary Stadtholder, William V of Orange-Nassau, and the aristocratic and pro-French 'Patriots'. In 1786-7 the Patriots had gained the upper hand, dramatically reducing William's powers in the process. William's wife was also the new Prussian King's sister and in June 1787 she was arrested by the Patriots after an initiative designed to gain extra support for her husband. She appealed for help to both Britain and Prussia. Had France responded in support of the Patriots, then war might have resulted. In September 1787, Pitt wrote to William Eden, British Ambassador in Paris, that if France wanted to retain 'predominant influence' in the United Provinces, it would need to '*fight for it*' (Ehrman, I, 534).

In fact, it was the Prussians who prepared to fight. After much delay, and diplomatic scurrying, they invaded Holland in mid-September 1787 in support of the Orangists. They captured Amsterdam the following month with no response from France. Britain's own firm line in support of the Stadtholder won it respect, however grudging, throughout Europe. It was widely recognised as symbolising the end of Britain's European isolation. The practical consequence was the emergence of a Triple Alliance with Prussia and the United Provinces during 1788. This took place in two stages. First, Britain and the United Provinces signed a treaty of mutual defence in April, by which they pledged to respect each other's territories. Second, once it had been clarified that Prussia was not interested in supporting British maritime adventures and that Britain had no wish to become embroiled in any central European conflicts with Austria, a defensive alliance with Prussia followed in August.

The third factor which changed the diplomatic situation may readily be inferred from the outcome of the Dutch crisis. It became obvious during 1787 that France's financial difficulties were of such magnitude as to reduce the country's effectiveness both at home and abroad. Britain still had ample reason to be wary of French intentions. France's trading interests in the West Indies, for example, had (like Britain's) been expanding rapidly since the end of the American war and a real likelihood of renewed conflict in the Caribbean existed. However, the financially stricken monarchy of Louis XVI no longer seemed such a threat to Britain's north European trade through the Low Countries. Nor did it look to form aggressive alliances with Spain and Austria. The deepening financial and political crisis in France increased Britain's room for diplomatic manoeuvre.

Trade

Pitt looked to commerce as the best means both of increasing national wealth and of reducing tensions between nations. Although it would be quite wrong to see William Pitt as some out-and-out free-trade liberal, an eighteenth-century precursor of the *laissez-faire* priorities of Gladstone or Richard Cobden, he had read Adam Smith's *Wealth of Nations* (published 1776) and found its general line of argument persuasive. He came to believe, like Smith, that national interests were not served by trade wars between countries which erected massive tariff barriers against the entry of each other's goods and employed the so-called mercantilist system which relied upon accumulation of precious metals as a measure of a nation's wealth.

It is not, therefore, surprising that trade negotiations took place with no fewer than eight European states – France, Spain, Portugal, Russia, Prussia, Holland, Poland and the Two Sicilies – in the years 1784–92. Few produced substantial outcomes but the importance Pitt gave them was a measure of his priorities. Following Smith again, he saw trade expansion within Europe as a means of making good the loss of the American colonies. Since other European nations were seeking commercial arrangements anyway, it seemed doubly important not to be left behind.

Much the most important outcome of this flurry of commercial activity was the so-called Eden Trade Treaty with France, signed in 1786. It was named after the principal negotiator, William Eden, an ambitious and highly controversial figure who had served in junior office under North in the 1770s and early 1780s and had been a close friend of Fox. He had also played a prominent part in parliament in helping defeat Pitt's proposals for a customs union with Ireland in 1785 (see Chapter 8). Pitt chose him as principal negotiator because he respected both his abilities and his knowledge of trade. He had been a member of the Board of Trade from 1776–82 and was also active in Indian commercial affairs. The fact that Carmarthen disliked him as a political turncoat and an intriguer probably only increased his attraction to Pitt. Carmarthen saw little value in the 'present Rage for Commercial treaties' which, he believed, would be likely to 'sacrifice our Political Weight upon the Continent' (Ehrman, I, 478). In truth, Pitt and Carmarthen had little in common and there is little evidence that the Prime Minister even had much respect for his Foreign Secretary's abilities.

The Eden Trade Treaty, though it promised more than time would permit it to deliver, was, for its time, a surprisingly thoroughgoing document. It gave subjects of France and Britain free access to each other's country without passports or any form of taxation. Freedom of navigation and trade between the colonies of the two nations was also established.

Tariffs were significantly reduced on a range of manufactured items, including textiles, hardware and cutlery. In what many in Britain considered a damaging concession, French wines were allowed into Britain at the same low rate as that levied on wines from Portugal, Britain's oldest ally. This effectively conferred 'favoured-nation' status on the French.

The treaty was heavily criticised, not least by Fox, who argued that the concessions were incompatible with Britain's traditional hostility to France as the major threat alike to Britain's commercial empire and to the balance of power in Europe. It was a view shared by some of Pitt's own ministers and by manufacturers wary of increased competition. Events proved most British fears groundless. The concession on French wines was of relatively little commercial significance, though it was appreciated by wealthy hosts and hostesses in London society, well used to providing lavish alcoholic provision for their guests. Lowered French duties on British manufactured goods, on the other hand, proved vital. Manufacturers of textile goods during the early stages of Britain's industrial revolution were given an opportunity which was eagerly seized. A hostile article in the *Daily Universal Register* in August 1786 had complained that 'England and France have the same manufactures, are vying with each other for competition' (Black, 1994, 111). What it overlooked, however, was the greater efficiency of British industry, and especially its more mechanised textile production, which meant that British exports were to become much more competitive in France than were their French counterparts in Britain. Furthermore, Pitt had insisted that French silk imports remained subject to heavy import duties. By the time the revolution broke out in Paris in 1789, it was clear that Britain had had much the better of the commercial bargain. Naturally, the outbreak of war with France in 1793 (see Chapter 6) destroyed the Eden Treaty. However, in the short time it was in operation it provided ample evidence of the values of trade liberalisation – at least to a country whose industrial revolution gave it an in-built competitive advantage.

Nootka Sound and Ochakov

Pitt faced two significant diplomatic crises before the outbreak of war. The one, though handled successfully, was of minimal long-term significance. The other, which had a less happy outcome, was also a harbinger of major suspicions and conflict which would resound throughout the nineteenth century.

The incident at Nootka Sound, off what is now Vancouver Island in western Canada, was born of Spain's desire to retain a substantial presence in North America. The country had long claimed rights over the entire western coast of the Americas, most of the northern part of which was entirely undeveloped and populated only by a few fishermen, traders and trappers. In July 1789, after a number of threats to trading vessels, the commander of a Spanish warship took possession of Nootka Sound, where a small British settlement had been established. It took almost eight months for the news from this remote region to reach Britain but the government's response was decisive. The Foreign Secretary wrote to the British consul in Madrid that the country would vigorously assert its 'complete right…to visit for the purposes of trade, or to make a settlement in the district' (Black, 1994, 234). Although diplomatic channels between Britain and Spain remained open during the few months the crisis lasted, it was clear that Pitt, confident in the support of parliament which voted appropriate supplies, was prepared to go to war. Crucially, Spain could no longer rely on any help from its ally France, now in the throes of revolution. It was thus forced to back down, allow Britain's claim and pay compensation. The government's response also involved a full mobilisation of the navy. As events turned out (see Chapter 6), this precautionary action was a valuable rehearsal for the real struggle ahead.

The Ochakov crisis brought Britain into dispute with Russia. Ochakov was a fortress on the northern shore of the Black Sea. Russia captured it after a siege in 1788 during a war with the Turks which lasted from 1787 to 1791. While negotiations for peace were in progress, the Foreign Secretary, Carmarthen, who had now inherited a peerage as Duke of Leeds, argued that the Triple Alliance should be invoked to put pressure on Russia. Leeds was anxious that the increasingly delicate balance of power in eastern Europe be not disturbed. Accordingly, in March 1791 he presented the Russian ruler, Catherine the Great, with an ultimatum. It demanded that, as part of the peace, Ochakov should be returned to the Turks. When Catherine refused to comply, the British government requested extra funds from parliament to equip the navy for an attack upon Russia. Parliament agreed to the request with a comfortable majority but Pitt quickly saw that parliamentary resolve was not so firm as it had been over Nootka Sound. Charles James Fox roused opposition forces with a splendid speech which played both on the widespread respect for Russia which existed in many quarters of British educated opinion, and on the lack of an obvious strategic benefit to Britain. Why risk war over an obscure place of which few had even heard until a few weeks before?

Perhaps more significantly, even those who *did* know about Ochakov queried both its importance and Pitt's judgement. In previous conflicts,

Ochakov had usually fallen quickly and it was clear that other fortifications were of far greater significance to the Turks. Writing from The Hague, Lord Auckland had asked Pitt in January 1791: 'I wish you would take occasion to...tell me your opinion of the real value and importance of Ochakov; both in respect to the Sultan's means of defence, and also with respect to the commerce of the Black Sea' (Black, 1994, 286). Convincing answers were difficult to marshal and Pitt was becoming uncomfortably aware that his alliance with Prussia was bringing Britain more closely into central European entanglements than had been intended when it was signed three years earlier. By April 1791, he was ready to countermand his Foreign Secretary's ultimatum and let Catherine keep Ochakov. As he explained in a letter to Joseph Ewart, the British envoy in the Prussian capital, Berlin: 'they [Members of Parliament] can be embarked in a War from motives of passion, but they cannot be made to comprehend a case in which the most valuable interests of the Country are at stake' (Ehrman, II, 24).

The price which Pitt paid was the loss of his Foreign Secretary and a certain loss of face. Leeds could not stomach being overruled on an initiative he considered vital to British interests. He was also concerned at the likely consequences of deserting Prussia. Pitt was content enough to see Leeds go. He had held the office since the beginning of Pitt's ministry and, in Ehrman's words, 'had long been a lightweight' (Ehrman, II, 26). In any case, Pitt was much closer both personally and politically to his cousin Grenville whom he rapidly advised the King to appoint in Leeds' place. Henry Dundas then replaced Grenville at the Home Office, leaving Pitt with able and trusted ministers in both the most senior government offices.

The loss of face was potentially more serious. For a time, having roused his supporters with effective speeches and having been supported by increasingly important newspaper opinion, Fox harboured thoughts of returning to office. He was never a man for the sustained campaign, however, and with Pitt's credit with the King far from exhausted, this was never a realistic possibility. Still, at the height of the crisis, Pitt considered resignation. He persuaded himself, however, that to resign would be to abandon the King, leaving him without an obvious successor and 'driving the Government...into a state of absolute confusion' while also (as he wrote to Ewart), shaking 'the whole of our system abroad' (Ehrman, II, 31). Having decided to ride out the crisis, Pitt survived a short-term propaganda blast from the opposition, not least because he showed the ability to retreat from what he quickly realised was an untenable position. Events as they unfolded in France over the next two years meanwhile quickly made Ochakov seem like a very small storm in a Balkan teacup.

Assessment

While Ochakov was a small storm in itself, some European diplomats recognised even then that it was also the harbinger of something bigger. From the perspective available to European observers in 1790–1 France appeared enfeebled by its revolution, possibly terminally. Meanwhile, Britain had recovered swiftly from its defeat in the American war to become a much richer and more confident nation in 1791 than had seemed possible eight years earlier. France's *ancien régime*, by contrast, had suffered first bankruptcy, then overthrow. The enmity of a century seemed to have been resolved in Britain's favour. Meanwhile, Russia, under the guidance of Catherine the Great, had become much more self-assured and aggressive. In particular, its challenge to Turkish supremacy in the Black Sea seemed to offer a new threat to Britain's commercial and strategic interests in the eastern Mediterranean. France had been the national enemy in the eighteenth century; there was every reason to believe that Russia would become so in the nineteenth.

Pitt glimpsed this possibility, but for much of this period he gave foreign affairs relatively low priority. Both his temperament and his interests inclined him to concentrate on domestic matters (see Chapter 3). He was also more interested in trade than in diplomacy. However, he provided decisive leadership when it was required. Having interested himself little in the growing links between France and Holland during 1785, he wrote a long and detailed memorandum of advice to Eden when affairs reached crisis point in Holland in 1787. His ideas clearly owed nothing to the advice of Carmarthen. He also took charge of negotiations with Spain over Nootka Sound and it was he who made the decision about when to undertake a judicious retreat over Ochakov. Neither decision pleased Leeds and the second, as we have seen, precipitated his resignation. During his peacetime administration, while Pitt gave only as much attention to foreign affairs as he judged necessary, his ultimate authority was never in question.

To what extent was Britain's stronger position in 1791 the result of clearly defined objectives pursued through effective diplomacy, and to what extent did it result from good fortune? Certainly, Britain *did* have effective ambassadors who kept ministers well informed and were highly respected abroad. Men like William Eden (Lord Auckland), Sir James Harris and Joseph Ewart promoted British interests well. J. Holland Rose, from a school of history writing grounded in decisive, unequivocal judgements, called the diplomacy of the last two during the Dutch crisis 'a marvel of skill' (Holland Rose, 1911, 381). The advice provided by Britain's senior diplomats was usually good. Had Auckland been heeded when he queried why Britain was taking such an exposed position on Ochakov, a damaging crisis would have been averted.

Nevertheless, the direction of foreign policy was not in strong hands. Carmarthen (Leeds) had a strong belief in alliance systems but he was neither a strategist nor an effective negotiator. In any event, he usually left the detailed work to others. When he did take a decisive stand, his judgement was usually faulty. The important alliances which were made in this period – with Holland and Prussia – were cemented more because of events which Britain did not command than because of effective diplomacy. Once it was clear that Britain had recovered from the American war and that, despite expectations, its economy had not suffered, it became a natural target for nations in search of allies. Getting Britain back into the frequently fluctuating pattern of European alliances was, therefore, a relatively straightforward process.

5

Pitt, Party and Monarchy

No 'party man'?

'I do not wish…to call myself anything but an *Independent Whig*' wrote the 20-year-old Pitt to the Earl of Westmorland in July 1779 (Ehrman, I, 17). His position on this never subsequently changed. Although his letter contained the important additional clarification: 'Which in words is hardly a distinction, as every one alike pretends to it', events over the next twenty-five years would make the 'distinction' important enough. Pitt's early indications of 'independency' from the hated Fox-North coalition were a prime recommendation for George III in the winter of 1783–4 (see Chapters 1 and 2). Like his father, Pitt was never a 'party man' in the sense of preferring party organisations, structures and policies hammered out in group discussions. He developed his own policies, presented them honestly and authoritatively to the Commons and expected good preparation and lucid presentation to sway the House to support his government.

Parliamentary majorities based on the success of cogent argument, of course, was the ideal. Practical politics required both the support of the King and at least a cadre of regular support in both houses of parliament. As Prime Minister in the early 1780s Pitt could rely on the unvarying loyalty of perhaps twenty-five MPs in the Commons. This was a far smaller number than the regular opposition of Fox and North, though it had been increased to about fifty by the end of 1788 after five years of successful government. His authority as Prime Minister depended much more upon the selection of competent subordinates, control of debate and support from a substantial section of the independent members than upon

*Indep. members.
debate control.*

any close party ties. This arrangement also suited Pitt's personality. Shy, often aloof and distinctly 'unclubbable' (in direct contrast to Fox), Pitt was not temperamentally inclined to that close linkage of politics and sociability which characterised natural 'party men' of the time.

The followers of Pitt, not surprisingly, began calling themselves 'Pittites' and, so long as Pitt retained the confidence of George III, it is not too far-fetched to consider them almost as a 'court party'. The impression of organised political activity is strengthened by the Pittites' use of newspapers to put their ideas sympathetically into the public domain – a well-established political ploy by the 1780s. Between 1776 and 1780 Lord North had used the *Morning Post*, under the editorship of the Anglican clergyman Henry Bate, as a 'ministerialist' journal providing pro-government propaganda and vitriolic comment about the rebellious American colonies. In opposition after 1783, the Fox–North grouping's 'house-journal' was the *Morning Herald*. To counter the anti-government, and increasingly democratic, material being produced in London in the early 1790s (see Chapter 7), the Pittites founded two newspapers, the *Sun* and the *True Briton* in 1792–3. Both were edited by John Heriot, whose efforts were liberally subsidised from Treasury funds (Sack, 1993, 12).

Political parties: image and reality

A good deal of political organisation took place under Pitt; we should certainly not consider that the so-called 'spin doctors' and 'image manipulators' of the late twentieth century had no precursors in late eighteenth-century Britain. However, this is not to claim that a fully-developed two-party system had emerged in British politics by this time, with Pitt leading the government party and Fox the opposition. It is still less valid to claim that Pitt was the Tory leader and Fox the Whig. Two main reasons explain why the period of Fox and Pitt has been presented as one of two-party conflict. One is historical and the other historiographical, and the two are linked.

It suited the Foxites, of course, to claim that they were the 'true' Whigs, the guardians of English liberties and inheritors of those benevolent men who had destroyed the monarchical despotism of James II in the Glorious Revolution in 1688. They characterised their opponents as 'Tories' – as late as the 1780s still a term of abuse for many – in the control of a malevolent monarch. For Foxite Whigs, George III was trying to destroy the liberties which Englishmen had won in 1688 and the younger Pitt was merely his dupe – doing the King's will to the damage of Britain. The Foxites thus tried to portray a Manichean struggle between 'good' and 'evil'. In this characterisation, Fox ('good') led a party which claimed the control of an elected parliament over the executive, concern for the liberty of the subject, and tolerance of diverse religious opinion. Pitt was notionally in charge of the government party but was in reality manipulated almost as a puppet by George III ('evil') who wanted to control parliament himself and trample on Englishmen's liberties. The 'evil' party also viewed the Church of England, usually opposed to such measures of religious toleration as the proposed repeal of the Test and Corporation Acts in 1787 and 1789, as a major prop to the King's potentially despotic 'system'.

This was, to be sure, a horribly crude characterisation but Fox believed much of his own propaganda. A more elegant and refined version of it, however, was to surface in nineteenth-century history books. One of the most gifted historians of that century was the Whig politician Thomas Babington Macaulay who served in Melbourne's cabinet in the late 1830s and early 1840s. His famous *History of England*, published between 1846 and 1862, never even got as far as the Whig supremacy which began with the Hanoverian succession in 1714. That did not stop its Whiggish views permeating historical interpretation for at least half a century. Whig history was essentially the story of progress and events were often selected and presented in ways which facilitated seeing the past as the story of a long and complex passage from a lesser to a greater state. It was history well attuned to an imperial age when Britain was the world's leading industrial power, when its navy ruled the waves and when about a third of the land mass of the globe was coloured pink to denote British 'ownership'.

It is easy to see how this way of looking at the past could present the 1780s and 1790s as an age of party. If history's purpose is to explain progress, with the implicit assumption that the current age represents ultimate progress, then those past events which most obviously relate to present developments are given disproportionate significance. In the long term, it is undeniable that the main change in Britain's system of government was that from monarchical rule to cabinet government with a parliamentary system. Ministers became responsible to parliament; the monarch's direct powers dwindled almost to nothing. Control of parliament depended on the outcome of a power struggle between two major political parties, each of whom competed for the approval of the electorate

Because all these changes came about over a long period rather than suddenly (for example, as a result of revolution), there is room for interpretation about precisely how they happened. In the Whig interpretation, George III was presented as a monarch who dictated policy and opposed necessary change. That, after all, is exactly how opposition Whigs in the

1770s and 1780s saw him. The Foxite Whigs of the 1780s can also be presented as acting like a modern political party. In order to defeat them, Pitt and his followers had to become a political party too. Thus the political struggles of the 1780s emerge in this historiography as between recognisably modern parties. The King, by supporting one of them (Pitt's), was staging a doomed rearguard action in defence of monarchical authority.

This characterisation contains elements of truth but it is too simple. Party was certainly important. Charles Jenkinson noted just before the general election of 1784 that 'Mr Pitt is at the head of one party and Mr Fox at the head of the other' (Hill, 1985, 153). Moreover, with the election decisively won, Pitt still found himself faced with a coherent opposition. It was unprecedented for any eighteenth-century group to retain out of office the support of about 130–40 MPs in the House of Commons as the Fox-Portland-North group did until, and beyond, the next general election in 1790. To a degree, it acted like a modern party but it was far less organised and disciplined. Not least, Fox, by far the most authoritative speaker on the opposition side, frequently absented himself from the House; he preferred gambling, carousing and socialising (not least with the King's dissolute eldest son, George, Prince of Wales) unless some big issue was under debate. He was hardly a 'leader of the opposition' in the modern sense.

It is also true that George III had substantial political influence. This he used in zealous defence of monarchical authority. He considered the outcome of the 1784 general election as vindication of his own strategy (see Chapter 2) at least as much as a victory for Pitt. He also remained, as he had been since the beginning of his reign, opposed to the very idea of party; he considered it a malign device for reducing his influence in the political process. George was in no sense a Tory; early in the nineteenth century he called himself 'an old Whig', identifying with Whig politicians who towards the end of the reign of Queen Anne had worked to place England more centrally within European diplomacy. He also asserted that his model as King was William III (1689–1702), the main beneficiary of the so-called Glorious Revolution.

He did believe, however, and with some reason, that opposition Whigs were anxious to hack away at the royal prerogative. This he was determined to resist. His early appointment of Tories, including some who had in the 1740s been sympathetic to a restoration of the Stuart monarchy ('Jacobites') was symptomatic of his commitment to having what he called 'honest' and loyal men serve him. He was also anxious to balance, and therefore, he hoped, neutralise the malign impact of party. But this was a far cry from direct interference in policy-making. As Linda Colley has noted, 'There was no marked upsurge of royal influence over the Cabinet after 1760, rather the reverse. And there was no dramatic rise in royal interest and initiative and imperial policy' (Colley, 1994, 207). George placed greatest store on having people he trusted in both his court and his cabinet. Once they were there, far from dictating policy, he relied on their judgement, interfering only rarely. In refutation of the Foxite Whig myth, George III was no narrow reactionary, anxious to see a return, if not to royal despotism, then at least to royal control over policy.

' polite, distanced and reserve

Pitt and George III

For most of their relationship, the King trusted the younger Pitt and gave him a pretty free hand. This was not because George specially liked him. The atmosphere between the two men was polite, distanced and reserved. In Ehrman's words, they had 'a guarded working relationship' (Ehrman III, 34). Pitt made few appearances at court and his social skills were not tailored towards polite small-talk with the privileged but politically insignificant. George gave Pitt generous support on most issues for three main reasons. First, Pitt had delivered him from humiliation, if not from chaos, in 1783–4. Second, keeping Pitt in office seemed the best way of keeping the hated Fox out of it, while Lord North had given up all rights to royal support by allying with Fox in 1783. Perhaps the most important reason for George's support, however, was his own interpretation of royal responsibility. He appointed ministers of his choosing. He then expected to keep them in office while they retained the support of parliament and did not jeopardise the interests of the state. Significantly, he made no effort to halt Pitt's administrative reforms, even though they would have a devastating effect on the independent powers of the monarchy in the nineteenth century (see Chapter 3).

In fact, Pitt and George disagreed on a number of important issues. The King did not like parliamentary reform or what to him were Wilberforce's wearisomely persistent attempts to abolish the slave trade. Pitt was annoyed when George joined the *Fürstenbund* on behalf of Hanover without consulting his ministers. George was equally angry when Pitt back-pedalled on Ochakov, thus handing a propaganda victory to Catherine the Great, for whom the King had little time (see Chapter 4). Pitt also chafed about the need to work with Lord Chancellor Thurlow, a special favourite of the King whom he would not be able to get rid of until 1792. During the French wars, also, there were numerous differences over both strategy and tactics. George became particularly

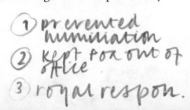

① prevented humiliation
② kept Fox out of office
③ royal respon.

anxious whenever Pitt seemed to be angling for a peace treaty with the French.

Both men recognised, however, that pushing differences into full-blown conflict was not in either's interest. For George, the always substantial spectre of Charles James Fox loomed; for Pitt, royal disfavour might mean loss of office. It is significant, for example, that Pitt did not present a fresh parliamentary reform bill after his rebuff in 1785 (Chapter 2) and that he soft-pedalled on a number of controversial measures in deference (at least in part) to royal sensibilities.

And yet the reason for Pitt's resignation in 1801 was royal disapproval. Pitt wanted Roman Catholic emancipation to accompany the Act of Union between Britain and Ireland (see Chapter 8); George would not have it. Why on this occasion did a difference of opinion lead to a fundamental rift, when so many earlier disagreements had been smoothed over? There are two main reasons. First, the King was rootedly opposed to concessions to the Roman Catholic Church. When a similar measure had been discussed in 1795, George had made his views known. He believed that having Catholics in parliament would bring about 'a total change in the principles of government...overturning the fabric of the Glorious Revolution'. His conclusion was unequivocal: 'I cannot conclude without expressing that the subject is beyond the decision of any Cabinet of Ministers' (Ehrman, II, 432). For the King, this was one of those rare constitutional issues which transcended normal political debate. The government had then not pushed the issue. George expected a similar response to a similar initiative six years later.

The second reason, however, gives an insight into the intensely personal considerations which often underlie great events. We have seen that Pitt had never been personally close to George. In 1799 and 1800, Pitt's always punishing work schedule took him ever closer to the edge of breakdown, and exhaustion seems to have warped his political judgement. He took the view that more important things weighed down a wartime prime minister than keeping the King abreast of the latest developments. His attendance at court, never overly punctilious, now slackened further. George felt slighted. The King did not want to dictate policy but he was sure that a monarch had the right to be kept fully informed about it, and comment on it. Dundas reported that the King now felt an 'aversion' to Pitt (Ehrman, III, 523). The mutual allegiances and accommodations of the past seventeen years became buried in recrimination. The King made his own position perfectly clear in a formal note written on 5 February 1801:

I had flattered myself that, on the strong assurance I gave Mr Pitt of keeping perfectly silent on the subject [Catholic Emancipation] whereon we entirely differ, provided on his part he kept off any disquisition on it for the present...we both understood our present line of conduct; but as I unfortunately find Mr Pitt does not draw the same conclusion, I must come to the unpleasant decision, as it will deprive me of his political service, of acquainting him that, rather than forego what I look on as my duty, I will without unnecessary delay attempt to make the most creditable arrangement [for a new government].

(Stanhope, III, xxxii)

Pitt resigned because he had lost the confidence of the monarch, not that of parliament. In a brief note beginning 'My Dear Pitt' – an unusual expression of intimacy from monarch to commoner in those days – the King brought himself to express his 'sorrow' but only in a sentence which made clear his expectation of the finality of the event: 'You are closing...Your Political Career' (Ehrman, III, 525).

The Pitt-Portland Coalition of 1794: the origins of a new Tory party?

Widely divergent responses to the French Revolution (see Chapter 7) finally shattered the unity of the Whig opposition. Lord North's own influence had anyway declined. He became blind in 1786 and attended parliament increasingly rarely before his death in the summer of 1792. Though the main opposition grouping led by Fox and Portland retained about 145 MPs after the general election of 1790, North's personal following had dwindled to insignificance. Of much greater importance was the division between those who, to put matters over-simply, believed that the French Revolution opened up genuine opportunities for adapting the old regime by embracing radical reform, and those who did not.

In the former camp were many of the younger Whigs, notably Grey, Sheridan and Whitbread. Crucially, although he strove hard to keep the party together, Fox declared that he believed reform to be the essence of Whiggery and Pitt's actions against personal freedom during 1792 forced him into siding with this group, despite his fears for party unity. In the latter, and substantially larger, camp were the Duke of Portland, Baron Loughborough, William Windham and the party's leading polemicist, Edmund Burke. It was Burke's famous *Reflections on the Revolution in France* (1790) which had begun the process of polarisation by indicating the fundamental evils to which, sooner or later, he believed the revolution must lead. Fox broke with Burke in 1791, after which a haemorrhaging of support began. Portland's position was critical. He rarely spoke in the House of Lords but he was an important political figure with a clear view of what the Whig party should stand for. In 1785, he had written to his son that he wished to see the overthrow of Pitt's government and its replacement by 'an administration composed of men of property and talents, who…are so united in principles and opinions as not to be led astray by popular clamour or royal favour' (Wilkinson, 1998, 251).

As early as January 1792, leading Whigs like Earl Spencer and William Windham were calling for the kind of restrictions on personal liberty to check the spread of 'French principles' (see Chapter 7) which were anathema to Fox. Pitt, well aware of the implications of Foxite divisions and alert to the opportunity for political advantage, began putting feelers out to Portland and North in the spring of 1792. The prospect of office for some disenchanted Whigs was enhanced by the dismissal of the Lord Chancellor, Thurlow.

These discussions came to nothing immediately but, as events in France had ever darker implications for the old order, it became clearer that Whig divisions would not easily be healed. In January 1793, Baron Loughborough (who had been a Northite) became the first from the old Fox-North grouping to join the Pitt government, accepting Thurlow's old post which Pitt had kept tantalisingly vacant for several months. Portland, however, still strove for party unity. After the war with France began (see Chapter 7), he urged that 'the best means of serving the public and the best chance of keeping a party together' was to offer 'cordial support to the war without any declaration of hostility to Fox' (Wilkinson, 1998, 255). In increasingly polarised times, this was an impossible task. However, the difficulties which Pitt experienced between 1792 and 1794 in attracting conservative Whigs into government is powerful evidence supporting the thesis that, in the 1780s, Fox and Portland had fashioned an organisation which resembled a modern party in many important respects.

Nevertheless, by July 1794, Pitt had succeeded in forming a coalition with Portland which 'might make us act together as one Great Family' (Ehrman, II, 409) against two closely related enemies: France abroad and the alarming spread of French principles at home. It was a genuine coalition. Six of the thirteen cabinet posts went to the Whigs, and Portland, in becoming Home Secretary, took one of the most senior positions. Portland also extracted from Pitt two policy concessions important to his grouping: clear commitment to the restoration of the Bourbon monarchy in France and movement towards greater religious toleration (Chapter 8) in Ireland. For private consumption, also, the Portland group looked forward to entering government in order to clean it up, and particularly to reduce royal influence. They were thereby able to remain true to a central tenet of Rockingham Whig faith (see Chapter 2).

Was it, however, a *Tory* coalition? The consensus of modern historical opinion is against seeing it as such. John Derry notes, quite correctly, that 'Pitt never ceased to call himself an independent Whig and those Whigs who had been recruited to his standard did not see themselves as abandoning their Whig principles' (Dickinson, 1989, 51). Frank O'Gorman, one of the leading supporters of the idea that modern parties evolved in the years before the 1832 Reform Act rather than afterwards, argued that

> The Coalition of 1794 and the series of events which led up to it... amount to a realignment of party loyalties and a reaffirmation of the strength of party in politics. The path to Coalition was a struggle less for office than for the soul of the Whig party and a battle for its future.
> (O'Gorman, 1982, 26–7)

He later affirmed that it was the Foxite Whigs who after 1794 'kept aloft the mantle of party' (O'Gorman, 1997, 257), suggesting that the Portland defection was intentionally into a wartime *coalition*, and did not represent a switch of allegiance from Whig to Tory. David Wilkinson's detailed researches into Portland's political career add further weight to the argument that we should see the Pitt-Portland government as a party realignment. Only a handful of the Whigs who joined Pitt in 1794 remained loyal to Portland when he formed his own government in 1807: 'Support for the Portland ministry was not based on those conservative Whig members who joined the coalition of 1794, and there had been no substantial accession of strength' (Wilkinson, 1998, 259).

All of this, however, may be to place too much emphasis on individuals and not enough on policy. Whatever labels politicians attached to themselves, it is difficult to dispute that a number of the issues at the heart of Tory politics in the second and third decades of the nineteenth century, when it was no longer a disadvantage to acknowledge the label 'Tory', came to the fore in the years after 1794. Some, interestingly, also harked back to a much older school of early eighteenth-century Toryism. The crucial issues were: belief that stable government could only be provided by those with property and education and not by 'mere numbers'; a strong preference for landed property as somehow more 'legitimate' than commercial, industrial or other forms of 'money-based' property; belief in monarchy as a vital prop to propertied government; support for a united

British nation against dangerous 'foreign' influences (see Chapter 7); support for the armed forces; belief in the supremacy of the Church of England (however much Pitt may have been personally indifferent to religion); and extreme wariness over, if not outright opposition to, any form of religious toleration.

Many of these beliefs owe more to Pitt, and especially to the 'Pittites' who followed him, than they do to the Whig tradition. This is one reason why Wilkinson calls the Coalition a 'Pittite triumph' rather than a 'genuine coalition' (Wilkinson, 1998, 247). They would not have developed in the way they did had it not been for the formidable strains placed on the old system by the French Revolution and by the wars with France which rapidly ensued. Those ideas, however, survived into the years of peace, and were at the core of Lord Liverpool's government (1812–27). They also survived into the allegedly modernising 'Conservatism' of Sir Robert Peel. If the Pitt-Portland coalition did not create the modern Conservative Party, it was nevertheless profoundly important in the transition to it. Perhaps we should conclude that the coalition was the midwife of modern Conservatism. As the present author has written elsewhere:

> The new Conservatism, as yet unrecognized in name and but dimly appreciated in concept, represented a fusion of party cohesion and careful administrative expertise, the legacy particularly of second-generation Pittites…most of whom entered politics in the 1790s and 1800s.
>
> (Evans, 1996, 63)

6

A Nation at War, 1793–1801

The causes of war

Britain did not go to war to stamp out the evils of a French Revolution which threatened to destroy the old political world. Far from it. The Revolution was initially welcomed by most of the political classes. Fox and some of his Whig allies saw it as the dawn of liberty. Pittites tended to view it more pragmatically. The Revolution would be an important distraction for Britain's greatest rival. Carmarthen, Foreign Secretary when the Bastille fell, wrote to the Duke of Dorset a fortnight later: 'I defy the ablest Heads in England to have planned, or its whole Wealth to have purchased, a Situation so fatal to its Rival, as that to which France is now reduced by her own intestine Commotions' (Ehrman, II, 4).

This reaction was slow to change. Even after Louis XVI's personal situation had become precarious, leading British politicians showed no inclination to intervene. In February 1792, Pitt's budget speech planned for reduced defence expenditure. The Prime Minister told the Commons, 'unquestionably there never was a time in the history of this country, when, from the situation in Europe, we might more reasonably expect fifteen years of peace than at the present moment' (Evans, 1996, 80). As late as November, when France had already been at war with Austria for almost seven months and with Prussia for more than three, the Foreign Secretary, Lord Grenville, urged Britain to keep 'wholly and entirely aloof' from European war (Dickinson, 1989, 128).

Had the main cause of war been ideological, then Britain would have become involved earlier than February 1793, probably in the spring or summer of 1792 in support of the Prussian monarchy or the Habsburg empire centred on Austria. Britain entered the conflict mainly for strategic and commercial reasons. Against general expectation, the French revolutionary armies had dramatic early successes against both the Prussians and the Austrians. The French defeated the Austrians at the Battle of Jemappes, just over the French border in the Austrian Netherlands (now Belgium), early in November 1792; eight days later a French army entered Brussels and then proceeded to occupy the whole of Belgium. This was an obvious threat to Holland, Britain's ally since 1788 (see Chapter 4). At the end of November France proclaimed freedom of navigation through the Scheldt estuary, contrary to treaties signed in 1648 and confirmed by both France and Britain in the 1780s. Pitt and Grenville immediately instructed Auckland, British envoy at the Hague, to tell the Dutch that there would be 'no hesitation as to the propriety of...assisting the Dutch Republic, as circumstances might require against any attempt to invade its dominions or to disturb its government' (Ehrman, II, 208). Though Pitt had noted a worsening situation in continental Europe since 1790, it is likely that this is the first occasion on which he gave serious thought to British involvement in the war. Revolutionary France now threatened the balance of power in northern Europe and its menacing presence in the Scheldt put commercial activity at risk also. Pitt told a French official in December 1792 that recent events in Belgium were 'considered as a proof of an intention [by France] to proceed to a rupture with Holland, that a rupture with Holland...must also lead to an immediate rupture with this country' (Black, 1991, 240).

Ideological issues played some part, it is true. Just as French troops were marching through the Low Countries, a new stridency and confidence was being heard from extra-parliamentary radical groups in a number of British cities (see Chapter 7). In the autumn of 1792, Burke cautioned that 'English assassins of the Jacobin faction...working hard to corrupt the public mind' were attracting increased support. In such dangerous times 'neutrality does not nor cannot produce neutral effects' (Black, 1994, 406). Since 1790, the government had considered Burke an alarmist, if not unhinged, critic; events across the Channel now finally persuaded the British government to agree with him. A propaganda effort against the radicals began. At the end of the year Auckland urged:

> every possible form of Proclamation to the People....The prosperity
> and opulence of England are such that, except the lowest and most desti-
> tute class, and men of undone fortunes and desperate pursuits, there are
> none would not suffer essentially in their fortunes, occupations, comfort,

in the glory, strength and well-being of their country, but above all in that sense of security which forms the sole happiness in life, by this new species of French disease which is spreading its contagion among us.

lacking plan/purpose

(Black, 1994, 423)

Desultory negotiations between Britain and France took place in November and December 1792. Some believed that war could be avoided since the French continued to assert that they had no fundamental quarrel with the British. More, including Pitt and Grenville, did not believe French protestations. Urgent preparations for war were finally put in train. News of the execution of Louis XVI on 21 January 1793 inflamed anti-radical passions in Britain. Bishop Horsley asserted that 'This foul murder, and these barbarities, have filled the measure of the guilt and infamy of France' (Black, 1994, 446). The fact that France actually declared war on 1 February was almost an irrelevance, though the declaration was accompanied by a call for the British people to rise in rebellion against their own oppressive government. Both sides by then knew that conflict was inevitable. Soon afterwards, the Duke of Leeds reported: 'we are here armed up to the teeth and the people in high spirits determined to defend the King and Country' (Black, 1991, 242). Pitt believed that the need for defence would be short-lived. Having failed to predict a war less than a year earlier (see above) he now spectacularly misjudged its *nature*. Britain was embarking on what would prove to be the longest war it had undertaken since the fifteenth century and much the costliest it had yet fought.

Strategy and outcome

Britain's attempt to defeat revolutionary France in the 1790s rested on three strategic pillars: supporting European allies, with cash and troops, in direct attacks on France; using the navy to pick off French colonies, especially in the Caribbean, thus weakening its commercial base; and offering practical aid and other forms of support to opponents of the Revolution within France. The first two of these had been tried and trusted during earlier wars with France during the eighteenth century and had generally been successful. Only in the American war, when France was able to concentrate its efforts on the Americas rather than having to worry about enemies in Europe, had Britain come off worse. The third strategy seemed a promising new ploy since it was well known that important areas of France, notably in the west, were resistant to revolutionary ideology.

In many respects, therefore, Pitt relied on the lessons of the past in tackling the struggle with France in the 1790s. The first need was to repel French advance in the Low Countries. It was reasonable to expect Austria (whose territory there had been invaded by France) to be a staunch ally in this objective. The so-called First Coalition against France, signed in February 1793, seemed particularly promising since it joined Britain to Austria as well as Prussia and Holland, allies since 1788 (see Chapter 4). Spain and Sardinia also came into the coalition, strengthening Pitt's original belief that the war would be a short and successful one.

The so-called 'blue water' strategy, which relied on Britain's naval strength and threatened French colonial possessions, was important for two reasons. Not only did it open up opportunity for fresh conquest by Britain; it also threatened to strike at the heart of France's own economy. Soon after the war began, Dundas, Secretary for War, spelled out the anticipated consequence: 'This country having captured the West Indian Islands and destroyed their existing fleet, may long rest in peace' (Dickinson, 1989, 150). Again, the emphasis on a short, successful war is notable.

In pursuit of the third strategy, Pitt also anticipated rapid success. Using Britain's Mediterranean fleet, Admiral Hood landed troops at Toulon in August 1793 at the invitation of the counter-revolutionary inhabitants there. Toulon was one of the most important ports in France. Pitt considered this a blow 'in every view the most important which could be struck towards the final success of the war' (Ehrman, II, 303), since it should lead to widespread insurgency against the revolutionary government, aided by Britain's European allies. This proved a false hope. As late as November 1793, Grenville was gloating that 'Every fresh account from France brings decisive proof that the system is drawing to its close' (Dickinson, 1989, 158). Yet the tide turned very quickly. Toulon was back in government hands by December and the British fleet withdrawn. A plan to land émigré forces on Quiberon Peninsula in southern Brittany in July 1795 had no more success. The unpalatable fact was that the French revolutionary forces were better prepared and had higher morale born of early success than had been expected. Worse, from the British point of view, was the clear evidence of national consciousness. Many in France preferred a Bourbon to a Jacobin government. They were all *French*, however, and most preferred a French government – almost any French government – to the restoration of monarchy engineered by the national enemy. Pitt and his ministers underestimated the power of French patriotism in the early stages of the Revolution.

Pitt also discovered that he could place less reliance on European allies than he had anticipated. There were many reasons for this. Austria and Prussia both had interests in central and eastern Europe which Britain did not share, not least the second and third partitions of Poland from which, with Russia, they gained much territorially in the years 1792–5. Russia's brief accession to the coalition in the Treaty of St Petersburg (1794) was of no practical benefit to Britain. Austria considered its possessions in Belgium geographically remote and difficult to defend. It was soon negotiating to have them swapped with the much more desirable territory of Bavaria in southern Germany. Britain had not had good relations with Austria in the 1780s (see Chapter 4) and the alliance which was forged out of necessity when Britain entered the war soon seemed an unnatural one. Both Austria and Prussia, furthermore, considered British support of their own efforts inadequate. They saw Britain as a rich nation, well able to afford the subsidies which would help equip and maintain them. Britain provided almost £66 million in subsidies throughout the war years but the subsidies were 'end-loaded'. Only about £9 million was spent on them in the years 1793–1802 (Sherwig, 1969). Pitt's war strategy has been much criticised, and with some justice (see pp. 51–2), but it is not fair to assert that he threw money recklessly at European allies. It is doubtful in any case whether there was enough to throw. Before the major tax reforms of the late 1790s (see p. 50), Britain had real difficulty in raising sufficient ready cash, even when it believed that the cash would be well spent.

Perceptions among the allies that Britain was the richest nation in Europe led to another cause of dissent between them. For Pitt, the security of the Low Countries was genuinely a vital matter. However, European diplomats well versed in eighteenth-century history knew of Britain's frequent preference for 'blue water' strategies and its lack of commitment to Europe. This was perhaps understandable when Britain was not perceived as possessing the most powerful economy in Europe, but Britain needed to be treated much more warily when that economy could, given the right circumstances, make Britain and not France the main threat to European stability.

These reasons explaining the fragility of the anti-French coalition need also to be set against the background of continued French triumphs in the field. Another pamphlet in this series deals with the Revolutionary and Napoleonic Wars. However, the speed and decisiveness of French success in Europe can very briefly be sketched here. Holland, which had a strong pro-French party anyway (see Chapter 4) was taken over in January 1795 and the country, which the French now called 'the Batavian Republic', declared war on Britain soon after. The Prussians and the

Spaniards made peace with France in April and July 1795. After signing an aggressive treaty with France in August 1796, Spain declared war on Britain two months later. Austria continued the fight, but crushing defeats in 1796 and 1797 forced it into a disadvantageous peace with France (at Campo Formio in October 1797) which recognised the Rhine as the eastern border of France. After this, Britain, alone of the European powers, continued the war against revolutionary France. A second coalition, involving Britain, Russia, Austria, Turkey, Portugal and Naples, was formed in the last days of 1798 but it proved to have even fewer unifying elements than the first; it, too, collapsed within a couple of years.

As usual, the British navy mitigated the effects of military disasters. Admiral Howe defeated the French fleet on 'the Glorious First of June' in 1794 but was unable to prevent vital grain consignments reaching western France. Other important successes were won during the crisis year of 1797 by Jervis and Nelson against the Spanish navy at Cape St Vincent in February and by Duncan against the Dutch at Camperdown, off the island of Texel, in October. The navy (with Nelson prominent) also played a crucial part in frustrating Napoleon's triumphant progress through Italy and North Africa in the years 1798–1801. Naval power also proved vital when an 'Armed Neutrality of the North' hostile to Britain was formed by Russia, Sweden, Denmark and Prussia in December 1800 in response to British claims to search all foreign ships and interfere with their trade. Nelson won yet another decisive victory in April 1801, this time against the Danish fleet anchored off Copenhagen. Despite severe initial difficulties over recruitment, refitting and shipbuilding, therefore, the navy had by 1801 virtually proved that, although Britain could make little or no impression on French dominance in much of western and southern Europe, it could defend the country against invasion while also helping to stifle the overseas trade of enemy countries.

This does not mean that the 'blue water' strategy was an unalloyed success. Its main thrust was intended to be in the West Indies, and against French colonial possessions. Here severe logistical problems were encountered. Britain had relatively little difficulty in capturing sugar islands and other places of strategic or commercial importance from France and, later, from Spain and the Dutch. In 1793–4, Tobago, the Seychelles, Martinique, St Lucia and Guadeloupe were all captured. Meanwhile, Jamaica, on which the French had designs, was successfully defended. In 1795–6, Ceylon, Demerara, Essequibo and Guiana were captured from the Dutch, Grenada from the French and Trinidad from the Spanish.

However, the successes Britain enjoyed outside Europe in the 1790s, especially in the West Indies, were won at a heavy price. Admiral John

Jervis and Lt Gen. Charles Grey were despatched to the West Indies in the autumn of 1793 with 7,000 troops. From 1795, when British troops were no longer of much use on the mainland of Europe, about half the British army was despatched to the Caribbean, where it was commanded by Sir Ralph Abercromby. Dundas was full of optimism. He told the commander in St Domingue in September 1795: 'You will be reinforced by an armament which…cannot fail to carry everything before it' (Ehrman, II, 567). He was wrong. According to Piers Mackesy's calculations, about 89,000 troops in all were sent to the Caribbean at this time. About 70 per cent of these were lost, mostly to various tropical diseases, notably yellow fever (Dickinson, 1989, 160). Meanwhile, the fighting capacity of France and its allies in the Caribbean was not destroyed.

Financial cost

The war, of course, blew all of Pitt's peacetime financial calculations (see Chapter 3) to smithereens. The national debt increased by about 80 per cent in the six years from 1792–8. The steady decline in the value of government stocks told of widespread investor anxiety as loans to the allies depleted reserves still further. For example, £4.6 million was loaned to Austria in 1795. Until 1797, Pitt levied no new taxes but the financial crisis of that year (which, along with the weary catalogue of defeats, threats of invasion and desertions by allies, brought him to the very brink of resignation) produced a change of approach. In February 1797 the government was forced to suspend cash payments by the Bank of England, forcing payments in 'promissory notes'. In the same year, he trebled the so-called 'assessed taxes' on luxuries like servants and carriages.

When the immediate crisis was over, Pitt took the crucial decision to fund wartime expenditure more by direct taxation than by loans. By early 1798, debt repayment had ballooned to almost one-third of all government expenditure, an intolerable long-term position (Ehrman, III, 259). Pitt's solution was to levy a new tax on income and to phase out the land tax, long hated by suspicious landowners who argued that 'the moneyed interest' had been unwarrantably advantaged by the tax system. Parliament was persuaded to sanction a 10 per cent (two shillings in the pound) tax on all income in excess of £200 a year from 1799, with lower rates from £60 to £200. It was the first 'income tax' in British history. The *Morning Chronicle* called it 'a daring innovation in English finance' (Ehrman, III, 262). It remained in force until 1816, though levied at lower rates from 1804–7, and it transformed the financial picture. It soon realised between £4 million and £5 million a year, and represented roughly 80 per cent of the value of all the new wartime taxes and about 28 per cent of all the extra money raised for the war in the years 1793–1815 (Dickinson, 1989, 183). That it brought in so much partly reflects the efficiency of the collection procedure. More importantly, it indicates the extent of wealth in British society available to be tapped over a long period to sustain the war effort. No other nation at the time could have levied so much or sustained such a draining conflict for such a time.

Assessment: how effective a war minister was the Younger Pitt?

Pitt left office before a lull in Anglo-French hostilities was agreed at the Treaty of Amiens in 1802. He had put out various feelers for peace himself since 1795 but they had got nowhere, partly because of divisions within the cabinet and royal disapproval, but mainly because before Britain produced a real check to French ambition at the end of Napoleon's Egyptian expedition, the enemy was not interested in negotiating anything other than a victor's peace.

The best that can be said about matters in 1802 was that Britain had not been defeated. For that it was disproportionately grateful for the efforts of its navy, although the ability of its middle and upper classes to raise large sums of money was also a significant factor. Pitt was not a victorious war leader. How much blame does he deserve for the failures of the 1790s?

Historians used to make a direct contrast between the Pitts, father and son. The Elder Pitt was characterised as a great war leader but an indifferent, and difficult, peacetime minister. The younger was praised for his administrative and financial genius in peacetime and for the 'national revival' of the 1780s over which he presided, but was dismissed as a 'disastrous' war minister. Both judgements are too crude. The Elder Pitt had a combination of favourable circumstances both in Europe and in the colonies which were denied to his son, not least a reliable and gifted ally in Frederick the Great. Also, the tenacity shown after 1797 when all the old allies had fallen by the wayside is worthy of the highest praise, and the Younger Pitt's determined leadership was important to this. Loyalist opinion rallied and a sense of national purpose was evoked. After a period in the early 1790s when government finance depended dangerously on loans (a policy Pitt himself regretted) he put national finances on a new, taxation-led, footing which carried it – just – through the remainder of a very long war.

It would, however, be foolish to assert that Pitt was a good wartime leader. A large number of basic errors were made which it is easy to identify, albeit with hindsight. First, Britain entered the war unprepared and undermanned. As Ehrman remarks, considering the situation in February 1793: 'The shape of that war itself had almost certainly not been considered. Neither Pitt nor anyone else appears to have given the matter close thought' (Ehrman, II, 261). Second, it took Pitt and his ministers too long to realise that their strategic concern with the situation in north-western Europe was not shared by Britain's main allies, Austria and Prussia. Austria, indeed, was prepared to exchange its territories in the Low Countries, and thus see Holland overrun, an outcome which ran clean counter to British interests. This basic misperception was an error of judgement which helped France to retain an advantage in the early stages of the war.

Third, Pitt believed for too long that the war would be short. His financial dispositions from 1793 to 1796 operated on this assumption. Much national wealth was wasted by inadequate early financing of a war which turned out to be very different from the one originally envisaged. Closely linked to this, Pitt was slow to react to the frequently rapid changes in 1793–4 and he seems not to have appreciated the need for more military and naval training. With some outstanding exceptions, Britain's commanders were not of the same calibre in the 1790s as they had been in the 1750s and they certainly could not provide instant success. Not until 1795 does it seem to have registered that the nation was in for a long haul, and with fewer advantages than it had originally calcu-lated. Pitt underestimated both the French fighting capability and France's sense of patriotic identity.

Fourth, Pitt was not decisive in arbitrating between conflicting advice. He could see the advantage of maintaining both a European and a colo-nial strategy (see pp. 46–7). In 1799, with the allies shown to be broken reeds, Dundas pushed strongly, first for outright victory in Egypt, whose occupation was 'the master key to all the commerce of the world' (Ehrman, III, 142) and then for British resources to be directed to areas of the world where France, and French trade, could be damaged. Grenville, on the other hand, believed that France would be defeated only in France. He wanted to channel more of Britain's land resources to an army which would support a renewed coalition when the time came. Pitt did not offer decisive leadership. Here, perhaps, his finely developed analytical skills were of least value. He knew that Britain held a poor hand and he could see different ways of playing it which might yield similar results. Experience had made him justly suspicious both of allies and of the opti-mism of French counter-revolutionaries. Not seeing an obviously preferable way forward, he usually exercised caution. It is possible that more visceral, and decisive, leadership would have paid higher dividends. In unpromising circumstances, a risk was probably worth taking but nothing in Pitt's cerebral make-up conduced him to gambling. He was a man whose career record until 1793 had been one of almost unvarying, and usually very speedy, success. Few such men take risks; they rely on their confidence and their abilities. Although Pitt acquitted himself well enough as Britain's war leader, the experience brought him face to face if not with defeat, then at least with the realisation that events were not his to command. It was a salutary lesson.

7

Pitt, Patriotism and Reform in the 1790s

*optimistic,
positive.*

The British radical tradition

I retain my opinion of the propriety of a Reform in Parliament if it could be obtained without mischief or danger. But I confess I am not sanguine enough to hope that a Reform at this time can safely be attempted....every rational man has two things to consider. These are the probability of success and the risk to be run by the attempt....I see no chance of succeeding in the attempt in the first place; and I see great danger of anarchy and confusion in the second.

(Stanhope, II, 152)

We cannot see without indignation, the attempts which have been made to weaken in the minds of his majesty's subjects, sentiments of obedience...and attachment to the form of government.

(Evans, 1996, 72)

These two statements, the first delivered by Pitt in the Commons in 1792 and the second from the Royal Proclamation against Seditious Writings issued in May the same year, sum up why Pitt turned against parliamentary reform. His intellectual preference for a more rational distribution of seats was overborne by fear of changing the old system when reform became associated in popular imagination with democracy, republicanism and attacks on privilege. Much the most important event triggering this association was, of course, the French Revolution. When, from early 1793, Britain was at war with revolutionary France, the need to protect British subjects from 'levellers', 'Jacobins' and 'atheists' also became a patriotic duty.

An authentic English radical tradition existed well before 1789, drawing its inspiration from the constitutional struggles with the Stuart monarchy in the seventeenth century. Not only was the tradition reformist; some of its supporters were democrats. In 1788, reformers held celebrations up and down the country to commemorate the centenary of the Glorious Revolution (O'Gorman, 1997, 242). Most did not do so in celebration of the *status quo* but to sustain the reformist impulse. They called, of course, for an increase in the franchise and a more rational distribution of parliamentary seats, but the reformist agenda did not stop there. It also encompassed attacks on the privileges and the conservatism of the Church of England; campaigns for religious toleration; and continued struggle against the 'unrepresentative' influence of monarchy and court. Much of it fitted readily into the Fox-Portland opposition agenda (see Chapter 5). Reformism was embraced by many in the middle ranks of society, especially nonconformists, professionals, writers and intellectuals; it also attracted a number of skilled and craft workers in London and other leading cities. It remained pretty clearly under the control of property owners and thus was thought to present no fundamental challenge to the authorities.

For a brief period in 1788 it seemed that the reformist agenda would be realised under a Whig administration headed by Charles James Fox. At the end of October, within days of the centenary of the arrival of the Prince of Orange (later William III) on English soil, George III endured his first sustained period of mental instability. For several weeks it looked as if George would be declared unfit to carry out his duties. A regency would be needed and the Regent could only be the King's eldest son, George, Prince of Wales, a crony of Fox and an opponent of Pitt. The opposition Whigs, who had always considered themselves the only true heirs of the Glorious Revolution, anticipated a fresh period in power when they could return to that reformist agenda unconstitutionally (or so they thought) snatched from them by a despotic monarch in December 1783 (see Chapter 1). Only the sudden recovery of the King saved Pitt's government.

The impact of the French Revolution

Initially, the French Revolution was widely welcomed in most quarters both as a decisive blow to Catholic absolutism and as a welcome check to the aggressive designs of Britain's most powerful enemy (Chapter 4). Within two years, however, the situation changed utterly. Organisations committed to democratic reform began to be formed by working people themselves.

The Sheffield Society for Constitutional Information was established in 1791 and the London Corresponding Society (LCS) followed in 1792. Both were run by artisans, both were committed to the pursuit of democracy and both sought, in the words of the LCS's rules, 'members unlimited'. The word 'corresponding' was to be taken literally. These artisan societies corresponded both with each other and with the French. They also published pamphlets and organised meetings designed to spread the word. By the end of 1792 a number of democratic organisations had been founded in most of the large towns in England and Scotland.

Their main inspiration was Thomas Paine, whose famous book *The Rights of Man* was published in two parts. The first, in 1791, was a rebuttal of the attacks on French revolutionary ideology mounted by Edmund Burke (see Chapter 5). Though not originally published in a cheap edition, it sold very well. Part I played a vital role in urging radicals to ground their case less on the corruption and illegitimate royal and aristocratic influence which had so stained the purity of England's 'ancient constitution' – essentially the Foxite position – and much more on 'natural rights', the distinctive political development of the European Enlightenment. Part II, published more cheaply in 1792, was dynamite. In addition to the arguments in favour of democratic government, the book mounted vigorous attacks on the very institution of aristocracy and on all forms of unearned privilege. It also contained specific proposals to improve the lot of ordinary folk: free education, family allowances and old-age pensions. *The Rights of Man* was a book which popularised the ideas of the European Enlightenment; it spoke directly and powerfully to self-improving skilled workers. Its message was advancement through merit, not accident of birth. It was, furthermore, patriotic to call for radical reform even in the face of opposition from the authorities using 'whips and racks' and erecting 'scaffolds'. As John Gale Jones, a leading member of the LCS put it, if with lurid metaphor: 'Are we Britons, and is not liberty our birthright....The holy blood of Patriotism, streaming from the severing axe, shall carry with it the infant seeds of Liberty' (Thompson, 1968, 154).

Pitt, therefore, faced an ideological struggle. Like all Whigs, 'independent' (as he called himself) or otherwise, he believed in government on behalf of the people but certainly not in government constructed by, or directly answerable to, the people. He was not opposed to reform but was certain that any reform should be controlled by the existing social and political elite. He believed that the existing political order was a force for good and that Painite radicals wished to overthrow it. The main differences between radicalism in Britain in the 1790s and its earlier manifestations were, first, that its focus had been widened and deepened by the example of France and, second, that the established social elites were no longer in control of the movement for reform. The Association of the Friends of the People formed by Charles Grey in 1792, was an attempt to assert common interests between the Whigs and the radical societies and to sustain the long-standing Whig commitment to reform. It could never control the direction of reform. What it was safe for an educated and propertied elite to debate in the 1780s became, especially after the outbreak of war in February 1793, unsafe and threatening when proposed by corresponding societies and other organisations supported by working people.

Repression?

Pitt's government moved swiftly against the threat posed by these new societies and by the publications they produced. Fresh legislation restricting freedom of speech, writing and assembly was passed in most parliamentary sessions from 1792 to 1801. In May and December 1792 two royal proclamations were issued against what were called 'seditious writings'. The Habeas Corpus Amendment Act was suspended from May 1794 to July 1795 and suspended again from 1798–1801. The practical effect was that the authorities could arrest anyone on suspicion of having committed a crime and detain them indefinitely without bringing specific charges.

Harvest failures and economic depression combined with increased political consciousness in 1794–5 to produce the largest amount of popular unrest in the decade. After George III's coach was attacked as the King went to open a new session of parliament in October 1795, Pitt introduced new legislation, the Seditious Meetings and Treasonable Practices Acts. Known as the 'Two Acts', the first prohibited the calling of political meetings without authorisation by a magistrate and the second defined treason so loosely that, as Fox sardonically observed, any politician advocating a measure of parliamentary reform – however mild – was liable to arrest under its provisions. In 1797, legislation was passed in response to two naval mutinies at Spithead and the Nore. It strengthened penalties for attempts to undermine allegiance to the authorities and administering unlawful oaths. In 1798 a Defence of the Realm Act was passed which required county-by-county information about the number of able-bodied men who would volunteer to defend the country. In 1799 and 1800, all forms of 'combination' by working men in trades unions were formally prohibited.

Did all of this amount to a policy of repression? Foxite Whigs certainly thought so, frequently complaining about the government's unwarranted attacks on personal liberty. They challenged the Two Acts almost clause by clause in parliament. Fox called for peaceful protest against them throughout the country in the form of petitions. More than 130,000 signatures were collected. An important school of history writing, including J. L. and Barbara Hammond before the First World War, G. D. H. Cole in the 1930s, and E. P. Thompson in the 1960s, has taken a similar line. For Thompson, the 1790s were the crucial decade in the process whereby working people discovered a distinctive voice raised in protest against the ruling elite on their journey to becoming an 'English Working Class' (Thompson, 1968). Even Pitt's sympathetic biographer called the Seditious Meetings Bill 'open-endedly severe' and the 'anger' with which the Two Acts were received 'real and widespread' (Ehrman, II, 456, 458).

There is overwhelming evidence, however, not only that government policies to secure public order and combat the threat of radicalism were strongly supported by the mass of propertied opinion, but that what might be termed 'popular conservatism' was a significant development during the 1790s. In many towns, loyalist associations attracted far more members than did radical ones. After 1794, armed volunteer companies were formed up and down the land. They attracted substantial support not only from landowners and the upper middle classes but also from far more modest property owners, such as small shopkeepers. Radicals were frequently the target of popular abuse and outright persecution, whether orchestrated by local magistrates or not. The Mayor of Nottingham, for example, encouraged anti-radical riots; he also authorised vigorous searches of houses occupied by radicals to trace incriminating evidence (Emsley, 1985, 821). The government developed a spy system which was increasingly active in rooting out disaffection. In 1795, according to Thompson, the LCS 'felt itself surrounded by spies' (Thompson, 1968, 179). Overall, however, Pitt's government can hardly be convicted of instituting a regime of terror – certainly nothing to compare with the activities of the revolutionary regime in France in the years 1792–4. Thompson nevertheless portrays its policies as malign:

> It has been argued that the bark of the Two Acts was worse than their bite. The death penalty was never exacted under their provisions.... It was, of course, the bark which Pitt wanted: fear, spies, watchful magistrates with undefined powers, the occasional example.
>
> (Thompson, 1968, 161)

The Duke of Portland was a strongly anti-radical Home Secretary after 1794, but his resources were severely limited. The Home Office staff did not exceed two dozen and Portland was heavily dependent on information coming to him from fearful loyalist magistrates. The government enacted repressive legislation but used it only fitfully. About 200 prosecutions for sedition were begun in the 1790s. This was certainly a larger number than in the 1780s but far fewer than in what might be termed the genuine reign of terror unleashed on the Jacobites during the rebellions of 1715 and 1745–6 (Emsley, 1985, 822).

The Two Acts were, of course, passed with huge majorities by the property owners represented in parliament. Only forty-five MPs voted against the Treasonable Practices Bill in the Commons and only fifty-one against the Seditious Meetings Bill. The government had no need to whip up support. Even with only about half the members actually bothering to vote, Pitt had majorities of around 200. Many property owners undoubtedly feared a revolution. Even the normally phlegmatic Pitt was concerned. After a meeting with him in November 1795, Wilberforce noted in his diary: 'I see that he expects a civil broil. Never was a time when so loudly called on to prepare for the worst' (Emsley, 1979, 48).

The Royal Proclamations against Seditious Writings in 1792 produced about 500 loyal addresses from towns up and down the country. These had clearly been signed not only by the magistrates, who had responsibility for public order anyway, but also by small property owners. Petitions from Bath, for example, had more than 5,000 signatures, those from Wakefield and Kidderminster 1,700 (Dickinson, 1989, 113). A government-sponsored society founded by John Reeves in 1792 'for the Preservation of Property against Republicans and Levellers' has attracted much attention from historians but it was only one of many such founded both to defend property and to meet the challenge of the French. Perhaps as many as 2,000 were established in the 1790s, organised usually by magistrates, Church of England clergymen and other property owners. As Dickinson suggests, however, ordinary people also gave their support:

> Although the lower orders do not bulk large in the organising committees, there is abundant evidence to suggest that they attended the initial meetings setting up these associations, engaged in subsequent loyalist demonstrations, and supported the loyalist addresses sent to the king.
>
> (Dickinson, 1989, 115)

Patriotism

Clearly a propaganda war was going on for the soul of the nation. In the 'conservative' camp the choice was simple. Was the country to be governed by educated, responsible, practical property owners and men of affairs or by those without any such experience whose heads were filled with 'theoretical speculations' and who, at best, had been misled and misguided by rabble-rousers and 'levellers' who took their marching orders from the country's major enemy? Though Pitt was obviously concerned with the overall propaganda strategy, played a major part in drafting the Royal Proclamations, sat on the so-called 'Committee of Secrecy' of 1794 which marshalled evidence of a 'Jacobin plot' against the social and political order which led to arrests of leading radicals, and took the lead in the campaign to secure the Two Acts at the end of 1795, he was not usually in charge of government propaganda. That he left to others, confident that support for the government's stand among property owners, and even among many below that level, was increasing as the war progressed.

Loyalist propaganda had two main objectives: to represent radicals as dangerous demagogues who were not to be trusted, and to wrest the use of the word 'patriot' from the radicals and appropriate it for the use of those who upheld the existing order. The most successful series of publications in the 1790s did precisely this. Hannah More's *Cheap Repository Tracts* were a series of commonsensical rebuttals of Tom Paine, written to be distributed by the gentry among their labourers. 'Will Chip' was Hannah More's fount of common sense. Chip easily refuted all of Paine's supposedly half-baked ideas and made ordinary folk feel grateful to be governed by such charitable and enlightened rulers. Her *Tracts* sold about 2 million copies, compared with 200,000 for the cheap edition of Part II of *The Rights of Man*. The Suffolk Curate William Jones called on John Bull, the mythical embodiment of Englishness, for the same purpose. His *Letters from John Bull* warned against radical politics. Radicals committed 'Treason to their King and Ruin to their country' (Evans, 1996, 53). One of the most successful pro-government periodicals was *Anti-Jacobin*, founded in 1798 and edited in its early years by the young George Canning, then Pitt's Under-Secretary at the Foreign Office. Its dominant theme was also patriotism as the proper response to French pretensions:

> For to thy Country's foes; 'tis Thine to Claim
> From Britain's genuine sons a British fame –
> Too long French manners our fair isle disgrac'd
> Too long French fashions shamed our native taste.

> (Evans, 1995, 226)

The King's profile was also raised. Until 1789 George III was a highly controversial figure in British political life. He was frequently vilified and in 1788 it was widely believed that he had gone mad. He was now reinvented and 'marketed' as a symbol of national unity. The old pictures, showing him as an overweight, bucolic figure with an uncomprehending stare and markedly lacking royal stature, disappeared except in radical cartoons. New, flattering, portraits of him were commissioned; they frequently depicted him as a calm, beneficent figure in military uniform. That by Francis Bartolozzi painted in 1800 has him in a gilt frame, surrounded by cherubim, upheld by Britannia, with the Union Flag as a shield, and guarded by a lion (Colley, 1994, 194). In 1797, George processed through the streets of London past a huge admiring crowd to give thanks in St Paul's Cathedral for important naval victories against the French, Spanish and Dutch (see Chapter 6). The anniversary of George's accession, 25 October, began to be celebrated as a feast day. Less flatteringly, but making the same point about national unity, the cartoonist Richard Newton portrayed the King and William Pitt as a single two-headed figure both staring steadfastly out against any enemy. The cartoon is captioned 'Head – and Brains'.

We may agree that British society became polarised as never before in the 1790s. Whether 'radicals' or 'conservatives' emerged victorious is more controversial. Radical apologists note that the case for parliamentary reform and attacks on 'corruption' took firm root among the lower orders in this decade. Despite widespread repression by local magistrates and by Pitt's hostile government, the flame of reform would never be extinguished. It would burn ever brighter until a radical Reform Act had to be conceded in 1832. For some, this was the beginning of a new age of 'class consciousness'. Other historians, increasingly numerous in recent years, see the anti-reformers as the decisive short-term victors. The nation responded patriotically. French ideas were both ridiculed and condemned; conservatism, no less than radicalism, became genuinely popular in this period. Certainly, after the legislation of 1795, radicalism was driven underground. It would not emerge as anything like a mass movement again until the last years of the French wars, almost a decade after Pitt's death. The years 1794–7 were crucial for Pitt. He fashioned a much stronger anti-radical administration and enacted legislation which forced radical politics to the margins of public life. After 1797, with radicalism in retreat and substantial naval victories at last to report, Pitt could concentrate his energies far more on raising funds to continue the war against the French.

1. Harmonius relations.
2. Trading empire after loss of USA.
3. 'Back door' for GB enemies.

8

The Importance of Ireland

Act of Union
– Catholic emancipation as an
addition.

Trade and Empire

We have already seen (Chapter 5) that Roman Catholic Emancipation, which Pitt wished to introduce as a necessary adjunct to the Act of Union between Britain and Ireland, was the occasion of his fall from power in 1801. Ireland, however, played a much more important role in Pitt's career than this. Three issues were particularly significant. First, he was anxious to establish harmonious relations with the Irish parliament. Ireland had achieved legislative independence in domestic affairs from Shelburne's government in July 1782 when the British government had feared a rebellion by Irish Protestant 'Volunteers', following the example of the American colonists. Second, Ireland became an even more important part of Britain's trading empire after the loss of America. The concept of Empire was increasingly important to the British ruling classes in the second half of the eighteenth century and Ireland was now at the very core of Britain's imperial identity. Furthermore, Pitt inherited considerable Anglo-Irish antagonism which posed a substantial threat to national recovery. Third, a discontented Ireland was an open invitation as a 'backdoor' for Britain's enemies. After 1793, Pitt's government had to be vigilant against plans for a French invasion using Ireland as a base.

The situation in Ireland was complex. Its population when Pitt came to power was 4 million, more than half the population of England, more than double that of Scotland – and growing rapidly. About 80 per cent of Ireland's inhabitants were Roman Catholic. Most of its land, however, was owned by Protestants, either absentee British aristocrats or the descen-

62 *protestant powe*

dants of the English and Scottish Presbyterian settlers of the seventeenth century. Among the Protestants, supporters of the Church of Ireland (the name for the Church of England in Ireland) were both socially and politically dominant. The increasingly prosperous cattle and linen trades were also Protestant controlled, and dislocations in the linen trade during the American war had been one of the main reasons for the formation of the Volunteers. Legislative independence after 1782 was, in practice, the privilege of perhaps 10 per cent of Ireland's population. What would soon be called the 'Protestant Ascendancy' was, in reality, an Anglican ascendancy. No Presbyterians sat in the Dublin Parliament. Catholics were totally excluded; they did not vote for the Irish parliament, nor could they sit as MPs in Dublin.

Henry Grattan, the radical Dublin lawyer who gave his name to the Irish parliament of 1782 – a misnomer since he never came near to controlling it – enthused about Ireland as a 'distinct kingdom'. Its allegiance remained to the Protestant Hanoverian monarch. Ireland would be 'inseparably annexed to the Crown of Great Britain' (Ehrman, I, 196). Grattan took it as read that this was a kingdom governed by, and primarily for the benefit of, its Protestant elite. The so-called 'Patriots' he led resented interference from Britain. They had some sense of Irishness but their identity was in no sense 'Gaelic' or Catholic. 'The political class continually emphasised their continuity of tradition and culture with England' (Foster, 1988, 252). Though its extent differed from region to region within Ireland, and though there were plenty of poor Protestants in the north of the country and some wealthy Catholics, especially in Dublin, grinding poverty was disproportionately a Catholic experience. Opportunities for Catholic advancement at a time of mounting national prosperity were limited.

'Pitt always saw England's Irish question as a problem of economic relations' (Foster, 1988, 253). This judgement is understandable from an Irish perspective but it is partial. Pitt took over discussions about the future relationship between Britain and Ireland which had involved North, Fox and Shelburne in the years 1779–83. All British statesmen agreed on the increased importance which Ireland now assumed within the empire after the departure of the American colonies. They were also agreed that Ireland, in addition to greater internal self-government, should have access to British trading markets at preferential rates. Out of the profits made by Irish traders, however, a contribution should be made to the defence of the Empire.

Pitt's interest extended beyond 'economic relations' because he placed such store on effective Anglo-Irish co-operation. He differed from his immediate predecessors, however, in the thoroughgoing nature of his proposals. These linked trade with both defence and the vested interests of the government in Ireland in an attempt to provide 'permanent tranquillity' there. Though no religious zealot, and temperamentally averse to discrimination, Pitt was prepared to consolidate Protestant domination in Ireland. He offered the Dublin parliament 'a prudent and temperate reform of Parliament' which would show regard 'to the interests and even prejudices of individuals who are concerned, and may unite the Protestant interest in *excluding the Catholics from any share in the representation* or the government of the country' (Ehrman, I, 200).

Pitt's proposals of 1785 in effect anticipated free trade between Britain and Ireland and, from the increased benefits which Irish traders would thereby enjoy, money for imperial defence. The theme of imperial strength was emphasised in his speech to the Commons:

> Adopt then, adopt that system of trade with Ireland that will have tended to enrich one part of the empire without impoverishing the other, while it gives strength to both... Of all the objects of my political life, this is in my opinion the most important that I shall have engaged in.
>
> (Stanhope, I, 267–8)

The Irish hated the idea of forcible contribution to the British defence budget, likening it ominously to George Grenville's ill-starred proposals to tax the American colonies in the 1760s. They also favoured positive discrimination in favour of their own products rather than free trade with Britain. British manufacturers were scarcely more charmed. A General Chamber of Manufacturers was formed in March 1785 to organise against what it saw as a new threat from Ireland, especially to England's wool trade. There was considerable irony in the fact that its first chairman was the Staffordshire master potter, Josiah Wedgwood, a political reformer and a man whose great fortune depended in no small measure on exploiting increased trade opportunities in Europe. Assailed on both sides, Pitt resentfully withdrew his proposals. Ehrman called this 'Pitt's most serious failure in his first two years in office' (Ehrman, I, 213). However, Anglo-Irish relations became more harmonious on the back of substantially increased trade in both countries. The value of Irish linen exports (mostly to Britain) trebled in the years 1781–92 while a protective Corn Law passed by the Dublin parliament further encouraged the production of Irish grain for British markets. It is significant that Dublin was willing to reduce its own tariffs to the levels agreed by the Eden Trade Treaty with

France (see Chapter 4) and also passed a Navigation Act in 1787 which closely mirrored the British Act passed a year earlier (Christie, 1982, 203). The Irish parliament was, however, prepared to use its independence on occasion. Its majority was closer to Fox than Pitt and, in early 1789, Dublin actually invested the Prince of Wales with the title of Regent while Pitt was desperately playing for time in London (see Chapter 7).

Radicalism and rebellion

As in Britain, the impact of the French Revolution transformed affairs in Ireland. It inspired reformers whose agenda went far beyond the cautious objectives of the Volunteers. Irish Reformers had two main objectives: an enhanced sense of separate national consciousness, and democracy. Neither remotely appealed to parliament in either London or Dublin. Nationalism, interestingly, was a non-sectarian cause in the 1790s. Two societies of 'United Irishmen' were founded in October and November 1791. The first was centred on Belfast and led by the Dublin lawyer Theobold Wolfe Tone; its first adherents were mostly Presbyterian and middle-class: drapers, linen manufacturers, shipbrokers and the like. The second, founded in Dublin by the ironmonger and land agent Napper Tandy, was predominantly Catholic. The societies had a common purpose. The Resolutions of the Belfast society roundly declared:

> That the weight of English influence in the government of this country is so great, as to require a cordial union, among ALL THE PEOPLE OF IRELAND....no reform is practicable, efficacious, or just, which does not include *Irishmen* of every religious persuasion.
>
> (Dickinson, 1989, 87)

These Irish radicals bought *The Rights of Man* as avidly as did their British counterparts (see Chapter 7) and they also imbibed its severely rationalist message. Noting that a key objective of the French revolutionaries had been the destruction of Church power, they aimed similarly to educate the people and reduce the influence of 'superstition' whether peddled by Anglican vicars or Roman Catholic priests. Converting an illiterate peasantry to sophisticated rationalist goals was a tall order and it is no surprise that poor Catholics in the rural areas should react to worsening economic conditions and food shortages with agrarian violence. Nor were they inclined to sacrifice a lifelong allegiance to their priests because of the power of Tom Paine's writing or the articles in *Northern Star*, the United Irishmen's newspaper, published from 1792–7.

By 1792 sufficient evidence of widespread disaffection in Ireland existed to sound alarm bells in Britain. Pitt and Dundas urged the Irish parliament towards concessions to the majority Catholic community which would 'keep everything quiet for a time' (Ehrman, II, 222). Pitt had responded to Catholic pressure in England in 1791 by promoting a Catholic Relief Act. This removed a string of obsolete penalties while enabling Catholics who took an Oath of Allegiance to hold a number of local offices and to practise as lawyers. He wished to see at least equivalent legislation for Ireland, though preferably in extended form given the size and disquiet of the Catholic majority there. He met with fierce resistance from the Protestant Ascendancy. The Chief Secretary, Robert Hobert, voiced the fears of many that political concessions to Catholics would upset the delicate balance in the country and threaten those upon whose loyalty the government most depended.

In the event, two Bills were passed into law, but not without much arm-twisting of members of the Irish parliament which left a sense of lingering resentment, even betrayal, within the Protestant Ascendancy. In 1792, Irish Catholics were permitted to practise law, to act as school-teachers and to employ apprentices in trade. After further agitation, the Act of 1793 allowed Catholics to vote in parliamentary elections and to hold a number of civil and military offices, although not the most senior or influential. Catholics were still not permitted to become members of parliament.

One more, highly controversial, attempt to loosen political restrictions on Roman Catholics was made in 1795. As part of the political deal brokered between Pitt and Portland in 1794, Earl Fitzwilliam, a Portland Whig who supported religious toleration, was appointed Chief Secretary of Ireland. His tenure of the office was brief. Despite promising the government in London that he would not remodel the Irish administration, he quickly sacked the influential anti-Catholic commissioner of revenue, John Beresford, and then clearly indicated his support for a new Catholic relief bill introduced into the Irish parliament by Grattan. Pitt, who during a brief lull in the agitation within Ireland had probably not been paying sufficient attention to how Fitzwilliam was operating, was forced to order his recall. He was replaced immediately by Pitt's close friend, the much more amenable Lord Camden. Pitt's handling of the Fitzwilliam affair was one of his biggest political misjudgements. He was open to Fox's accusation that it represented 'the most insulting display of the dependence of the Irish legislature' and proof of the country's 'state of degradation' (Evans, 1996, 100). It also alienated moderate reformers, who considered Fitzwilliam's recall as a betrayal of trust. Many Catholics now calculated that they had no alternative but to support the United Irishmen.

When popular agitation mounted in 1795 and 1796, Pitt was forced to give full support to the Protestant Ascendancy. The Fitzwilliam episode is a significant factor in the events which culminated in the Irish rebellion of 1798 (see p.68).

Measures of Catholic relief could anyway not solve the major problem of growing disaffection in Ireland. From 1793, when Britain went to war with France, the volume of correspondence between Irish radicals and the revolutionaries in Paris mounted alarmingly. Meanwhile, secret societies of Catholic 'Defenders' and Protestant 'Peep o' Day boys' perpetrated numerous rural atrocities. Conflict between these sectarian societies grew and in September 1795 an offshoot of the Peep o' Day agitators formed themselves into the Orange Order. The Order celebrated the triumph of the Protestant William III (William of Orange) over the Catholic James II at the Battle of the Boyne in 1690 and was dedicated to sustaining Protestant supremacy by almost any means. From 1795, it was clear that – to the horror of men like Tone – sectarianism had replaced rationalist radicalism as the dominant force in Irish popular politics.

From Pitt's perspective, however, the main danger from the mid-1790s was not sectarianism but French invasion of Britain from Ireland. This was Tone's objective in direct negotiations with the French Directory to support an Irish rebellion against British control. In December 1796, more than 14,000 French troops were sent under the command of one of the republic's best generals, Lazare Hoche. The expedition foundered on a combination of bad luck (including devastating storms in Bantry Bay) and bad planning. The United Irishmen were insufficiently ready to offer the support the French thought they would receive, which led to mutual recrimination. Nevertheless, the very size of the French commitment (one of the largest expeditionary forces of the war) was indicative of the importance they attached to it. Too late, as it turned out, the expedition gave heart to the United Irishmen, whose numbers and menace alike increased.

The British government took over responsibility for pacifying Ireland, though the brutal work of General Lake in Ulster in 1797–8, using predominantly Irish militia, was almost certainly counterproductive. Its efficient spy system penetrated many plots and hampered preparations for rebellion, especially in the south of Ireland. Nevertheless, the United Irishmen were able to mount some kind of insurrection, albeit disjointed, poorly co-ordinated and weakly supported by local communities. During May and June 1798, four separate outbreaks took place, around Dublin and in County Antrim, County Wexford and Connacht. Government troops dealt capably with each of them and the insurrection's leaders,

Henry Joy McCracken and Henry Munro, were among the 1,500 executed as part of severe reprisals. Significantly, when a French force led by General Humbert surrendered to the authorities at Ballinamuck (Co. Mayo) in September, the authorities accepted the French surrender peaceably, but they massacred about 2,000 Irish supporters of the rising. Tone, arriving in Ireland with a small force in September long after the main action was over, was captured and took his own life before he could be executed. United Irish bitterness and hostility to the British did not die with him.

Union

The immediate occasion of Pitt's decision to end the life of the Irish parliament was the insurrection of 1798. The very day after he heard of the first rising, he enquired of Camden: 'Cannot Crushing the Rebellion be followed by an Act appointing Commissioners to treat for an Union?' (Ehrman, III, 170). However, the insurrection only furnished ultimate proof that the Dublin parliament could not provide the order and tranquillity necessary for British, as well as Irish, security during a bloody war. A number of earlier issues had progressively destroyed the Prime Minister's faith in the constitutional experiment begun in 1782. It might be argued that the rebuff of his trade and defence proposals as far back as 1785 sowed the seeds, despite the fact that they were rejected in London as well as Dublin. Certainly, when discussions on the country took place, he was inclined to refer to 'the unlucky Subject of Ireland' (Ehrman, II, 430–1). A politician accustomed to success is prone to linger over failures, and their lessons, less than might be wise. So with Pitt and Ireland. He had large schemes for sustaining an imperial vision based on mutual harmony and reciprocity between the two countries. When these were baulked, his reactions were often less than generous or constructive.

His patience with the Ascendancy had worn thin before 1795 and events between 1795 and 1798 were profoundly disillusioning. He believed that a more flexible administration would have prevented the growth of mass support for the United Irishmen and that a better informed one would have been in a stronger position, if not to head off, then at least to deal effectively with the constant threat of French intervention. As it was, far too much of Britain's increasingly stretched resources were being put into the defence of Britain's back door when they could have been more effectively deployed in Europe, North Africa or the Caribbean. There is no reason to doubt that Lord Cornwallis's withering contempt for the Ascendancy after he took over as Lord Lieutenant in 1798 was shared by Pitt himself. When he addressed the

Commons on the subject of legislative union in January 1799 his condemnation of the old order was apparent: 'I say also, that much of the evil which Ireland now labours under, arises unavoidably from the condition of the Parliament of that country' (Ehrman, III, 182).

The major obstacle to political union, of course, lay not in London (where only twenty-five votes were cast against it in the Commons) but in Dublin. Far too many political careers, patronage appointments and opportunities for advancement within the Protestant Ascendancy were at risk for there to be anything but the strongest opposition. Pitt overbore it using not the methods of a reforming administrator or statesman but what US politicians would later call 'pork-barrel' politics. Using the enthusiastic talents of a new Chief Secretary, the young Irishman Viscount Castlereagh, and the much older Lord Lieutenant, Lord Cornwallis, Pitt bribed the Dublin parliament into surrendering its authority while attempting to conciliate the Catholic majority with talk of further concessions, and perhaps even the full emancipation which had been denied in 1793 and 1795 (see p. 66).

Grattan's commentary on this is well known:

> How did they pass the Union?
> By perjury and fraud;
> By slaves who sold their land for gold
> As Judas sold his God.

(Ehrman, III, 187)

But he protested too much. In truth, Cornwallis and Castlereagh were only using against it the self-same methods of patronage and acquiescence which had cemented not only Grattan's parliament but those which had preceded it. Nevertheless, the cost was high. Thirteen new Irish peerages were created – many of them going to men uncommitted to Union, though not usually openly hostile – and four British peerages were bestowed on Irish peers. Since only 100 Irish seats in the lower house were transferred to Westminster, many boroughs had to be disfranchised – at an average cost to the British exchequer of £15,000 per seat and a total cost of £1.5 million.

Opponents of Union fought a tenacious battle but an issue which had produced virtual dead heats in January 1799 was producing parliamentary majorities in the forties in early 1800. The Act of Union, creating 'a United Kingdom of Great Britain and Ireland', received the royal assent in July 1800 and came into operation on 1 January 1801. In addition to the 100 MPs in the Commons, the Union added twenty-eight peers and four bishops to the House of Lords. The system of government and administration for Ireland was largely retained, with a Chief Secretary, appointed by the Crown, acting as chief executive. Last-minute concessions saw some tariffs remain while the Irish exchequer was not united with the British until 1816.

The key unresolved issue, of course, was Catholic Emancipation. Cornwallis was known to be sympathetic while, in Britain, Pitt and Dundas both believed that a Union without emancipation would remove one of the pillars most likely to secure the loyalty of the majority population in Ireland. Pro-Union politicians in Ireland were generally careful to avoid promising emancipation, though many Catholics inferred it to be a likely consequence. The King's position, however, was well known (see Chapter 5) and, apparently, implacable. Since Pitt could not be sure of a majority for emancipation within his Cabinet, the King's resolve was never tested. Ireland's fate was to remain yoked for more than a century in a Union that became increasingly, and violently, unacceptable. Pitt's vision of a harmonious and genuinely 'United' kingdom was stillborn.

9

The Closing Years, 1801–6

Out of office

Pitt was out of office from March 1801 to May 1804, during which time Henry Addington held the office of Prime Minister. Although Addington was held in high regard by Pitt, who had first recommended him to the King as a sound replacement when he considered resignation during the dark days of 1797 (see Chapter 6), George's appointment of the Speaker of the Commons excited much ribald comment. Addington was considered as a political lightweight. Snobbish aristocrats also poured scorn on his middle-class origins by calling him 'the Doctor' (his father's occupation). Fox saw the appointment as further proof that the King still pulled the strings and controlled the executive. The ever-waspish George Canning coined a characteristically cruel put-down of the new Prime Minister in the journal *The Oracle*:

Pitt is to Addington
As London to Paddington.

(Stanhope, IV, 60)

Pitt hoped that the political transition would be smooth and he had no intention of criticising the incoming ministry. He took comfort from the fact that the new government contained a number of his own men, who intended to follow broadly 'Pittite' policies. Among the heavyweights, Portland remained, though quickly reshuffled from the Home Office to the less important office of Lord President. The strongly anti-Catholic Lord Eldon, who had been Pitt's Attorney General, now became Lord Chancellor. Pitt also welcomed two promotions from the younger generation of his ministers: Hawkesbury (from 1803, Lord Liverpool) became Foreign Secretary immediately, while Castlereagh (see Chapter 8) came into the mainstream of British politics as Secretary of the Board of Control in 1802. Such personnel seemed to justify Pitt's intention to give 'the fullest Support to the Formation and to the Ministers of any Administration composed of Persons acting upon the same General Principles as I had done' (Ehrman, III, 552).

In truth, things were not so rosy. Though it could hardly be foreseen at the time, Pitt's resignation inaugurated a damaging period of political instability which would encompass five ministries in eleven years. This instability remained until Lord Liverpool, reluctantly appointed Prime Minister by the Prince Regent in 1812, was recognised as secure at the very end of the Napoleonic Wars. The root of the problem, which grew during the next decade, was the division which opened up when Pitt resigned. His two right-hand men, Dundas and Grenville, also went out of office with him. Both were by 1801 supporters of his Catholic Emancipation policy. Pitt's apparently secure government had therefore, in practice, split between pro- and anti-Catholics. Most of the former group left office in 1801; most of the latter stayed on with Addington. As 'Pittites' increasingly accepted the label 'Tory' after Pitt's death, the Catholic question continued to threaten cohesion and party unity long after their master's death.

Pitt's period on the backbenches was brief but eventful. The first major issue on which he had to take a stand was the peace terms being negotiated by the new government and which became the Treaty of Amiens in 1802. This was severely criticised by those most opposed to revolutionary France. Their reasoning was simple: Britain had fought a long, expensive and arduous war, winning numerous colonial possessions in the process. Addington's peace returned them all, with the exception of Trinidad and Ceylon, in exchange for what its opponents considered only paltry concessions by the French in mainland Europe. Windham, in particular, was apoplectic at the new government's supine negotiating stance. Pitt's old Foreign Secretary, Grenville, called it 'most miserably defective...an act of weakness of humiliation' (Ehrman, III, 558). At least in public, Pitt remained loyal to his successor. He admitted to disappointment on strategic grounds that the Cape of Good Hope had been handed back to the Dutch. For the rest, he suggested to the Commons that the peace refrained from humiliating either of the main parties and was 'prudent'.

As such, it might prove a lasting settlement which also protected Britain's essential security (Ehrman, III, 563).

Pitt's public judgement was rapidly proved wrong, of course. Britain returned to war with France in May 1803 and, from that point, the clamour grew for him to return and lead the nation. Even during the brief peace, however, Addington's ministry was being sniped at by many of the old Pittite connection. The most important of these was Grenville who, with his equally impatient brothers, could not wait to bring Addington down. Pitt's reluctance to be stampeded into action, no less than his Olympian position that he would consider returning to office only as Prime Minister and only in response to the clearest summons from King and country, caused considerable friction with his old ally.

Addington was aware that his position was weakening. He was not a good speaker himself and his ministry could muster only limited debating talent. He retained important advantages. He could normally count on secure majorities in the Commons, he retained the confidence of the King, and he suffered no loss of support in the general election of 1802. Nevertheless, he felt vulnerable, particularly as the peace seemed more fragile with every passing month. He was perhaps more sensitive than he need have been. He used the breathing space afforded by the brief peace wisely. Britain returned to war in 1803 much better prepared and more securely defended than had been the case in 1793 (see Chapter 6). Addington's control of financial strategy suggested overall competence, though Pitt's forensic skill revealed his lack of understanding of the precise detail. Above all, Addington felt uncomfortable with Pitt's presence on the sidelines. This was understandable. The two men had had a warm relationship for much of the 1790s, but never one of equality. Pitt patronised the Speaker of the Commons, though never maliciously or probably even intentionally. Unable to convey authority or command in the Commons, Addington was sure that most political insiders considered him at best a passable stop-gap. At one point in 1802 he even suggested that Pitt return as Prime Minister while he remained in a senior, but subordinate, capacity. Pitt refused to countenance the idea since it would smack of 'backstairs dealing', would annoy the King and would certainly demean his own reputation as national leader. Out of office, Pitt seems to have become more sensitive about his reputation and his place in history. He contrived to give the impression that if the call to office were to come again, it would have to come from a weightier figure than 'Doctor' Addington. Relations between the two men inevitably soured and Pitt's original pledge to maintain support for the new ministry began to be tested. During 1803, he adopt an increasingly 'oppositionist' stance.

The return of war and the return of Mr Pitt

The resumption of hostilities with France quickly weakened the Addington administration. Soon the vultures were hovering. Fox, long absent from the Commons, began to stir himself again. The Grenvilles continued to scheme for Addington's downfall, and moved ever closer to an alliance with Fox and his supporters in order to achieve this objective. Addington himself was conscientious but dull and the absence of patriotic orators on the government benches in time of war told against him. Support from independent MPs began to drain away. By contrast, Pitt was making inspiring wartime orations. In a speech to the Commons on 22 July 1803, Pitt used apocalyptic tones to rouse parliamentary opinion to the continuation of a war which had already demanded so much:

> We must recollect…what it is we have at stake, what it is we have to contend for. It is for our property, it is for our liberty, it is for our independence, nay for our existence as a nation; it is for our character, it is for our very name as Englishmen, it is for everything dear and valuable to man on this side of the grave.

Only Pitt's reluctance to mount open opposition kept Addington in office in the autumn and winter of 1803–4. Once again, Grenville suggested to Pitt a direct assault on a 'manifestly incapable' government (Mitchell, 1992, 207). Once again, Pitt refused to take the bait. By January 1804, however, he had devised his own personal strategy. He decided to attack Addington on the subject of defence in general and naval administration in particular. His parliamentary attacks had the desired result and by March it was clear that the ministry could not survive. Government majorities, previously secure, began to dwindle alarmingly in both houses. As often happened when change was in the air, the number of MPs turning up to record their vote in big divisions increased and majorities in the twenties when 400–50 MPs were voting in the Commons were not enough to provide political security in wartime. By April 1804 it was clear that Addington was preparing to give up the prime ministership. For a time, he harboured hopes that Pitt would find a place for him in a reconstituted ministry, but was quickly disabused. He did, however, receive the salve of a peerage, becoming ennobled as Viscount Sidmouth.

What kind of ministry would replace Addington's was the subject of much speculation and gossip. Grenville, Fox and their supporters had made most of the running against Addington during 1803 and now hoped to reap their reward. Pitt was able to capitalise on his own hard-earned public reputation as guardian of the nation's interests in both peace and war. He had also regained the support of the King. As the Earl of Moira reported, with these advantages, Pitt would 'never be subordinate in any Cabinet' (Ehrman, III, 639). Nevertheless, he seems genuinely to have wanted to lead a broad-based administration. The prospect of a wartime coalition including, if not Fox, then certainly Fox's supporters as well as Grenville, in addition to most of those who had served in his previous government, had a strong appeal. He produced a long memorandum in which he argued for a 'comprehensive system' (Ehrman, III, 654).

The King, recently recovered from yet another bout of mental instability, blew Pitt's scheme apart. He threatened to withdraw any offer for Pitt to head an administration if Fox, or even Fox's men, came into government. Grenville had now moved so close to Fox that both he and his supporters considered such a precondition unacceptable. If Fox could not come in, neither would the Grenvillites. Forced to make a choice between forming a government with a narrower base than he wished, or considered wise, and rejecting the King's commission, Pitt chose to take office on the King's terms, rather than press his own and prolong ministerial uncertainty. The Foxites interpreted his decision as yet one more example not only of the King's political influence but also of Pitt's subservience to it. They interpreted Pitt's overtures to them as mere duplicity. They were wrong. Pitt's need for a broad-based administration exactly matched his desire to form one. He knew that the ministry he formed in May 1804, based on his old supporters, but shorn of Grenville and his friends, was likely to be weak. A week later Napoleon Bonaparte declared himself Emperor of the French and prepared to wage aggressive war. He was determined to rectify the one significant setback to French plans in the previous decade: a successful invasion of England. The tone of Pitt's second administration was already set. *came into ministry in bad curcs → not on his own terms. → french wanted to invade England*

Coda in a minor key

John Ehrman calls Pitt's last administration 'An Impaired Ministry'. It is a fair assessment and one which Pitt himself would almost certainly have accepted. His last twenty months in office, in truth, were an unworthy coda to what had gone before. His ministry was never secure at home. In foreign affairs, the unceasing search for allies seemed to have been successful, only for one of them to suffer among the most crushing and decisive of Napoleon's victories.

As we have seen, Addington's ministry had not been particularly talented. Shorn of the support of the Grenvillites, Pitt could not fashion a significantly stronger one. Even his personal direction seemed to count

insecure

Impaired → weakened

for less, not least because his health – never robust – had been giving rise to growing concern since the turn of the century. From the old ministry, Addington (now Sidmouth) departed; Portland, Camden, Eldon and Westmorland remained. So, for a time, did Dundas (who had been ennobled as Lord Melville in 1802). The younger Pittites were represented by Castlereagh (at the Board of Control), Hawkesbury (Home Secretary) and, chafing in minor office as Treasurer of the Navy, George Canning – the most talented, but the most disenchanted, of them. Both Hawkesbury and Castlereagh were poor speakers and the new Foreign Secretary, Lord Harrowby, was not much better. The new ministry did not lack for level heads and administrative ability but it was short of good debaters. It also lacked either weight or experience in the most senior positions. A revived and embittered opposition faced it unpersuaded of the need to continue the war and ready to criticise Pitt's policies for their lack of judgement and extravagance. *- Low -*

By the autumn of 1804, Pitt's Commons majorities were sometimes in the twenties or thirties, hardly larger than Addington's when commentators had begun to predict his overthrow. Parliamentary arithmetic and the fact that, as Camden put it, an uneasy government seemed to be able only to 'scramble thro' the Business of the Country' (Ehrman, III, 717) lay behind Pitt's reluctant decision to invite Sidmouth back into government. With him came Lord Hobart (Secretary for War in Addington's government and now succeeded to his father's peerage as Earl of Buckinghamshire). Pitt was anxious not so much for these less than starry names than for the thirty or so parliamentary votes they brought with them.

Even these votes were won at a heavy price. Sidmouth failed to support Pitt in early 1805 over accusations of financial impropriety levied against Viscount Melville. These resulted from detailed enquiries about malpractice during his unusually long tenure – 1782–3 and 1784–1801 – of the office of Treasurer of the Navy. Melville had never been popular in parliament. He was, for one thing, an able Scot at a time when the combination aroused suspicion, or worse, in England (Colley, 1994). Furthermore, his heavy-handed control over most of the forty-five Scottish MPs was widely resented. His many detractors thus considered him a particularly juicy target. A rather sordid affair, which the Foxite Whigs in general and Samuel Whitbread, one of their most trenchant orators, in particular enjoyed, ended with Melville's trial by the House of Lords. He was not to be acquitted until 1807, long after his enforced resignation from the government, which took place in May 1805. An enfeebled and internally divided ministry lacked the power to keep one of its most effective, though tainted, ministers in office.

It is a measure of the paucity of talent available to Pitt that Melville was replaced by Lord Barham. As Charles Middleton he had been a distinguished naval administrator in the 1780s, but he was now 78 years of age. Melville's abilities, if not his personality, were sorely missed. Even the choice of Barham was not without damaging consequences. Pitt had refused to appoint Sidmouth's favoured candidate, Buckinghamshire, to the vacancy. Sidmouth was further annoyed that, since Barham was a relative of Melville, the appointment might suggest to backbenchers evidence of inadequate government contrition. The consequence was that both Sidmouth and Buckinghamshire resigned, leaving Pitt by the autumn of 1805 no more favourably placed on the domestic front than he had been in January.

If events at home were uncomfortable in the autumn of 1805, those abroad were little short of disastrous, at least on the European mainland where Napoleon's troops were again rampant. Pitt's foreign policy was dominated, as in the 1790s, by the need to find reliable allies in the struggle against France. This was a laborious, and frequently frustrating, process. Allies were always likely to demand more than Pitt was prepared to give and he knew, from bitter experience, that they could readily be prised apart by an aggressive enemy. So it proved in 1805. The year had begun promisingly. After much diplomatic scurrying, an alliance with Russia was signed in April. By it, Tsar Alexander I promised to raise half a million men and Britain agreed, yet again, to provide subsidies for the allies. In August, Austria joined the coalition, though its price – a £3 million subsidy from Britain – meant a further 3d (1¼p) on the income tax.

Money, however, could not buy victory. The late summer and autumn saw an almost triumphal progress by Napoleon's armies through central Europe. Napoleon had already accepted the throne of Italy in May and he annexed Genoa the following month. In late September, he crossed the Rhine and in October the Danube in search of the Austrian army under General Mack. He defeated it at Ulm in late October and, yet more decisively, at Austerlitz at the beginning of December. Pitt's alliance system fell apart almost immediately. Austria signed an immediate armistice with France. Prussia, which had been negotiating a treaty with Russia to come into the war against France, now pulled back and, before Christmas, signed an alliance with Napoleon. Both British and Russian troops were in retreat.

As so often, salvation – or, as it must have seemed to Pitt at the end of 1805, welcome respite – came at sea. The one beneficial consequence of Pitt's alliance strategy was that Napoleon was forced to withdraw troops massing near Boulogne for an invasion of England and put them into combat against Austria. This fatally unbalanced his plans. The day after his victory at Ulm, these lay in ruins after Nelson's famous destruction of the Franco-Spanish fleet off Cape Trafalgar. On one reading, therefore, the fateful year 1805 ended in stalemate. British subsidies notwithstanding, Napoleon's grip on continental Europe appeared unshakable. However, the British navy had secured the British Isles against invasion. Britain could at least enjoy the bleak luxury of preventing total Napoleonic victory. It was difficult, however, to see how this essentially defensive achievement could be converted into a British victory.

Undoubtedly, the events of the year placed yet more strain on Pitt's fragile constitution. He had long been prone to bouts of sickness and to gout severe in a man of his age. Always a copious drinker, and frequently drinking alone, his resort to port and madeira now, both for their forti-fying and their analgesic properties, only made things worse. In December 1805, he was at fashionable Bath, taking the waters for their allegedly restorative properties. They failed to restore. By early January 1806, he had summoned his personal physician, Dr Walter Farqhuar, who found him 'much emaciated, very weak, feeble & low' (Ehrman, III, 821). Confirmation of the Austrian defeat at Austerlitz, which did not reach Pitt until 3 January, seemed to have exacerbated the stomach and bowel prob-lems which dogged him for much of his adult life.

His return to London took four days and weakened him still further. By mid-January his doctor's concern had turned to alarm; those closest to him began to realise that he was not likely to recover. His friend and old tutor, Bishop Tomline (whom Pitt had only recently failed to have elevated to the Archbishopric of Canterbury, in another demonstration that, in religious matters, George III's preferences and prejudices could still override the views of a Prime Minister) wanted to administer holy communion on 22 January but Pitt refused, saying that he lacked the strength. Pitt's own religious faith was never prominent; a later age might have categorised him as agnostic. It is not clear whether, *in extremis*, Pitt was evading the religious issue. Whichever, Tomline's offer of the rite demonstrated clearly enough that all hope had gone. Some of Pitt's last day was spent in dictating a will. Characteristically for a man whose private life was often spectacularly disorganised, such a document had not been compiled before. The younger Pitt died in his sleep during the early hours of 23 January, at the age of 46 years and 8 months. For more than two-fifths of his life he had been Prime Minister of Great Britain.

Assess the achievements

10

Conclusion and Assessment

Pitt and contemporary opinion

Pitt was 46 years old when he died. He had been directing the nation's affairs almost to the end and the extent of his rapid decline had not been widely reported. News of his death therefore came as a great shock. Grey and Canning were only two leading politicians, from opposite ends of the Westminster spectrum, who were aghast when they heard. When the Speaker of the House of Commons announced consideration of a proposal to erect a memorial to him 'The silence was death-like, and several of the hardiest oppositionists said it was like an electrical shock upon the House, and that they could hardly breathe' (Ehrman, III, 830). His old rival Charles James Fox, whose own death would occur less than eight months later, was reported as finding 'something missing in the world – a chasm or blank that cannot be supplied'. He had doubtless temporarily forgotten the cruel judgement he offered when told the previous month that Pitt was very ill. He 'should be very sorry to have Pitt escape in such a manner from the complete disgrace that must at last befall him' as a result of fundamentally misjudged policies. He refused to vote for the Commons motion to pay off Pitt's personal debts because the motion included the judgement that Pitt had been 'an excellent statesman'. If the motion

> had been proposed to remedy these pecuniary difficulties which Mr Pitt had incurred in the course of his political life – if it had been proposed to do those things for his relations which his own acknowledged

disinterestedness did not allow him to do…I would most willingly consent that all this should be done in the most liberal manner.

(Stanhope, IV, 392)

Within the Westminster circle, Pitt was respected by political friend and foe alike. In a letter written to her son on the day of Pitt's death, the Duchess of Devonshire repeated the by now standard Whig charge that Pitt came into office only on the illegitimate authority of the King but her enthusiasm for his use of the spoken word was unstinting:

Mr Pitt's fault as an Englishman and statesman was that he came into place against the constitution and supported himself in place by exercising the power of the throne'….'his eloquence was so great he could explain even ev'ry disaster into almost the contrary.' His choice of words was perfect, his voice beautiful, and his way of putting aside the question when he chose, and fascinating the minds of men, extraordinary.

His old Cambridge friend, and would-be conscience, William Wilberforce, commented on his

clear and comprehensive view of the most complicated subject in all its relations…fairness of mind which disposes a man to follow out, and when overtaken to recognise the truth; magnanimity, which made him ready to change his measures when he thought the good of his country required it…willingness to give a fair hearing to all that could be urged against his own opinions…personal purity, disinterestedness, integrity.

(Ehrman, III, 844–5)

We should not be entirely blinded by views expressed immediately after an unexpected death. The Foxites may have grudgingly respected Pitt's abilities but they were usually happy to blacken his character. Not only had he kept them out of office for years; they believed he had done so by being subservient to a King who threatened the constitution. He was no true Whig and not to be trusted. Private correspondence about him could be caustic. For Grey, Pitt was 'a mean low minded Dog'. For Fox, he was 'not a man capable of acting fairly & on a footing of equality with his Equals' (Mitchell, 1992, 213).

The radical press (see Chapter 7), was no more charitable. One of the most gifted of spokesmen for the poor was William Cobbett, whose *Political Register* became the most popular and influential radical journal of the day. Until 1804, Cobbett had been a Tory. The dyspeptic assessment which he wrote a week after Pitt's death may owe something to the zeal of the recent convert to radicalism. It certainly conveys a sense of Cobbett's own self-importance, which only expanded with age. Cobbett does, however, suggest (as did an increasing number of radical writings) that an evaluation of Pitt's contribution may depend on one's own place in the social hierarchy.

> That he may be regretted by those who were looking up to his power for emoluments, or for *shelter*, by the numerous swarm of 'blood-suckers and muck-worms'; that his loss may be regretted, and deeply regretted by these, I am far from meaning to deny; but that he is regretted by the *people of England* is a falsehood which, come whence it will, never shall pass uncontradicted by me.

In the course of a letter written to Pitt in October 1795, one of his many attempts to dissuade Pitt from concluding a peace with France, Edmund Burke praised the Prime Minister's 'much manly exertion' and declared: 'Everything is arduous about you' (Stanhope, II, 321). We cannot know whether Pitt was the more irritated by yet another lesson from Burke about the Satanism of French revolutionaries or gratified that one of the great political minds of the age recognised in him a characteristic he would most have prized: self-sacrificing labours in the national interest.

He was not so self-sacrificing as to resist defence of his honour by duelling – the conventional, but increasingly controversial, manner of settling disputes between gentlemen. Pitt fought a duel on Putney Heath with the Foxite Whig George Tierney on 27 May 1798 after an unpleasant interchange in the Commons during which Pitt had accused Tierney of having 'a desire to obstruct the defence of the country' (Stanhope, III, 129). It may seem incredible that national leaders should even think of submitting themselves to the haphazard outcome of bullet shots at twelve paces – especially during a war. It certainly offended Wilberforce's sense of propriety. He had to be strongly persuaded against introducing a bill into parliament against the principle of duels the very next week. However, codes of honour cut across conventional criteria of prudence and wisdom. It is worth remembering that, in much more recent times, only the personal intervention of King George VI prevented Winston Churchill from accompanying allied troops landing on the Normandy beaches in June 1944, an expedition which could easily have ended the then Prime Minister's life.

anti-reformer; patriotic

The Pitt legacy

For almost a generation after Pitt's death, many eagerly appropriated the title 'Pittite'. This partly reflected genuine regard for a great man. Those he promoted to high office, especially from the early 1790s onwards, held him in almost universally high esteem. The Earl of Liverpool, for example, who had served Pitt loyally since 1793 and who would be Prime Minister from 1812–27, almost as long as his mentor, was unstinting in his admiration. He wrote in 1814 that he always 'endeavoured to make the Principles of Mr Pitt the chief guide of our Political conduct' (Sack, 1993, 89). Others used the description not because of any particular policies but because Pitt had come to symbolise both steadfast opposition to France and 'French principles' and also support for the old order. A Pittite, therefore, was a patriot and an anti-reformer. By ironic extension, also, since Pitt was one of the least openly devout or 'religious' prime ministers of the eighteenth or nineteenth centuries, a Pittite was a supporter of orthodox religion as a secure shield against 'Jacobinism and Atheism'. Many 'Pittites' held reactionary views which would have made Pitt himself squirm with embarrassment.

Pitt's legacy is also measured in his concern for administrative efficiency and executive expertise. Government became more professional under him; his was a working administration. He did not mount a frontal assault on the patronage system, which was prone to give unmerited advancement to the inefficient if loyal, but he starved it of oxygen by promoting on merit where possible and by not replacing mere sinecurists. In doing so he paved the way for both Peel and Gladstone, whose nineteenth-century governments both earned a justified reputation for professionalism and attention to detail. Pitt also neatly avoided one of the main traps of 'party governments' in the 1780s. His parliamentary majorities, unlike theirs, were usually grounded in the support of his fellow ministers and the votes of backbenchers and independents keen to applaud cheap government and debt reduction. Again, both the concern for cheap government and the determination not to be led by party subordinates, presages the ministries of Peel and Gladstone.

The next Prime Minister of the first rank, Sir Robert Peel, was born in 1788 and did not enter parliament until 1809. He was thus not old enough to have learned at first hand from Pitt but he certainly copied his prime ministerial style. Like him, he took care to develop a cadre of ministers he could trust to do an efficient job and aimed to get business through parliament by mastery of debate. He was also prepared, if a clash could not be avoided, to put what he considered to be the national interest above party concerns. This explains the collapse of the Conservatives over

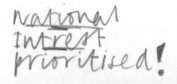

national interest prioritised!

the repeal of the Corn Laws in 1846. For Gladstone, Ireland became the great moral cause to which, if necessary, the unity of his own party might be sacrificed.

Pitt and the historians

History has, in general, treated Pitt kindly. Earl Stanhope, who collected together many of Pitt's political papers and speeches and linked them with an extensive commentary published in 1862, was unstintingly and, it has to be said, uncritically generous. Everything from Pitt's statesmanship and judgement to his relations with his servants comes in for praise. Here, in lifting the veil on some smaller matters, he contrives even to make adverse criticism into praise:

> The goodness and gentleness of Mr Pitt to all those who were any way dependent upon him formed a feature of his character. To his domestics his indulgence was indeed carried to a most faulty extreme, since he did not, as he ought, control their expenses or review their accounts. To the poor families around him he was ever ready to stretch forth his helping hand.
>
> (Stanhope, IV, 404)

Another of his early biographers was the Earl of Rosebery, himself a Prime Minister – though for a very much briefer period (1892–5). His assessment was similarly unequivocal:

> Pitt was endowed with mental powers of the first order; his readiness, his apprehension, his resource were extraordinary; the daily parliamentary demand on his brain and nerve power he met with serene and inexhaustible affluence; his industry, administrative activity, and public spirit were unrivalled; it was perhaps impossible to carry the force of sheer ability further.

J. Holland Rose's famous two-volume biography of 1911–12 is a strong representative of the school of 'Whig history', both in its tendency to intersperse narrative and analysis with moral judgements and confident statements about 'the needs of the age'. It is 'Whig' also in its tracing of 'progress' – in this case, the progress from the confusion and demoralisation of 1783 to the stronger, more secure government provided by Pitt:

> the younger [Pitt] helped to retrieve the disasters brought on by those who blindly disregarded the warnings of his father. In the personality of both father and son there was a stateliness that overawed ordinary

mortals, but the younger man certainly came more closely into touch with the progressive tendencies of the age.

(Holland Rose, 1911, 32)

Sir Arthur Bryant, writing in *The Years of Endurance* against the background of World War II, was similarly laudatory but stressed Pitt's practical abilities rather than his vision:

He was the parent of more practical reforms in administration and political economy than almost any other English statesman ....But he approached them with his eye, not on the horizon like a man of the study, but always on the treacherous and broken ground at his feet.

History writing in the second half of the twentieth century tends to eschew grand judgements in favour of reappraisals grounded in a more detailed study of archival and published material. It is also happier dealing with specific issues of interpretation than in painting broad confident canvasses. Broad-brush evaluations, at least about political leaders now long dead, have gone out of fashion. Thus, historians have recently been less concerned with whether Pitt 'saved the nation' in the 1790s and more with specific issues, such as whether Pitt's refashioned administration of 1794 (see Chapter 5) can be considered as the first 'Tory' administration of modern times, or whether Pitt's policies and attitudes *did* fundamentally change as a result of the French Revolution. Moral judgements, when found at all, derive disproportionately from history writing which emphasises change generated 'from below'. This school (whose heyday was in the 1960s and 1970s) replaced confident certainties about the work and characters of the great with equally confident (and, frequently, equally misguided) generalisations about the growing popularity of radicalism and how 'the working class' came into being. This school represented Pitt as an apostate to the reform he had embraced in the 1780s. His policies in the 1790s are presented unequivocally as 'repressive' of the liberties of Englishmen, with working people...forced into political and social *apartheid* during the [French] Wars (which, incidentally, they also had to fight). Pitt's 'system' represented corruption and reaction (Thompson, 1968, 491, 217, 507).

Reality, as so often, refuses to conform to such confident simplicities. As we have seen, what has been presented as Pitt's 'repression' in the 1790s was widely popular, and not merely among the propertied classes (Dickinson, 1989; Colley, 1994). The latest assessment of Pitt argues that his opinions underwent no fundamental shift in reaction to events in

84

France but that he was astute in following changes in public opinion. His transition to anti-radicalism was both 'reluctant' and delayed. In his attack on the radicals in 1794 (see Chapter 5) Pitt was no convert 'to the canons of counter-revolutionary conservatism'. Rather he invoked national unity 'to justify a war effort whose diplomatic and military parameters had changed dramatically since 1793'. Pitt 'did not spend the 1790s or any other decade of his life in perpetual fear of the lower orders' (Mori, 1997, 273, 275). For Mori, Pitt was far from an ideologically committed Prime Minister. In so far as he thought in abstract terms, he did prefer 'conservative concepts of social harmony to theoretical natural rights models' favoured by Enlightenment thinkers. However, and perhaps surprisingly, he found much to agree with in Tom Paine's vision of man as a rational, improving creature, if very little in the practical changes to which it pointed.

Ehrman's monumental three-volume biography provides the most detailed account of Pitt's career which we are ever likely to possess. It is full of fascinating detail and it is certainly not without adverse comment. Ehrman, for example, presents Pitt as a loner who expected loyalty from supporters and who felt that he deserved the approval of the nation for putting the nation's finances on a more robust footing and for his clear-headed direction of the war. His famous 'efficiency', however, depended on a clear, and arrogant, perception of priorities. In the papers discovered on his death, for example, were found examples of letters and memoranda, some up to twenty years old, to which he had never bothered to reply. These included many from the King, who frequently complained that Pitt would not write letters even to him. The Younger Pitt's legacy, indeed, included the largest (and most disordered) in-tray in British history.

His private finances were in a similar state of disorder. It is easy to present such disorder as symptomatic of Pitt's personal sacrifice to the higher national good. The truth is more complex. Pitt was, indeed, 'married to his work'. No Prime Minister (with the possible exception of Margaret Thatcher) put in more single-minded hours. Gladstone, who certainly contributed as much, had a significantly broader religious and intellectual hinterland than Pitt. Pitt was fascinated by finance and by ideas about trade and he enjoyed working with figures. As Ehrman puts it, 'he understood the language the experts spoke, and the circumstances in which the active economic forces of the country moved; as they in turn... recognised that they had a knowledgeable minister in Downing Street' (Ehrman, III, 845). At least in part, however, Pitt devoted himself to work because he found personal relations difficult. Even such a notoriously shy and glacial figure as Robert Peel had warmer relations with professional colleagues than Pitt and was also more at ease in the company of women. Pitt was awkward in many social contexts and found personal relations difficult. He was as infrequent an attender at Court as he could get away with, partly because he found its concerns ineffably trivial and beneath him, partly because the need to make small-talk exposed a raw inadequacy in him. The failure to marry almost certainly reflected similar unease. He seems rarely to have been happy and, like many who are similarly circumstanced, he resorted too readily to compensatory drinking. This, combined with a less than robust constitution, contributed to his premature demise.

Ehrman's biography, for all its myriad insights, is relatively reticent with the broad picture. Pitt's legacy is presented in characteristically prosaic terms:

> He gave a modernizing tone to the practice of government…that was well suited to current needs, and in more developed form because a part of the mental furniture of political generations in which the Blue Book [the name given in the nineteenth century to a detailed parliamentary investigation and report] came to replace the pamphlet of his own youth.
>
> (Ehrman, III, 845)

Presented in this light, it is very easy to see how Peel and Gladstone, like more immediate successors such as Liverpool, could be considered 'Pittites'. Pitt's concern with finance also fits contemporary historiographical analysis of eighteenth-century Britain which has traced its development as what John Brewer calls 'a fiscal military state'. Pitt's apparent fixation on finance is entirely explicable in this context. It is more controversial, however, to see a party political legacy. This book has argued (see Chapter 5) that the Pitt-Portland coalition is important in the transition to modern Toryism. So, in another context (see Chapter 7) was the appropriation of 'Patriotism' to the political status quo. Other historians are more sceptical. They point to the difficult, and fractured, transition to Toryism during the early nineteenth century when 'Pittites' frequently fell out among themselves, especially on religious policy.

There is also no reason to believe that Pitt saw party in these 'modernising' terms. He held fast to the description 'independent Whig'. This, it is true, was politically convenient since it offered no threats to the King, whose dislike for tight-knit party groupings was rooted and implacable. Pitt was technocrat first and politician a long way second. He certainly did not eschew the black arts of political management and propaganda. He contributed articles to Canning's *Anti-Jacobin* (see Chapter 7), for example, albeit on finance. However, he usually left political management to his subordinates, fixing his gaze from the mid-1790s on the war and on financing the war. He was a formidable performer, almost never worsted in parliamentary debate and nearly always on top of the business which he considered most important.

Pitt's deliberate preference for the title 'independent Whig', which many Foxites contemptuously rejected and which some historians have seen as precious and anachronistic, is also revealing about his political priorities. He was not a 'party man'. Both his temperament and intellectual convictions militated against close party connection. He was pragmatic rather than ideological, believing that the mastery of a political or economic brief counted for more than adherence to 'grand and speculative theories'. He also shunned what he considered the wasteful, debilitating and unnecessary links between political allegiance and social connection which were meat and, especially, drink to the Foxites.

His management of the war can be, and has widely been, criticised for its over-optimism in strategy and its many failures of tactics (see Chapters 6 and 9). However, no convincing case has emerged on how things might have been better managed overall, not least given the novelty and strength of the forces arraigned against Britain by French revolutionary armies and, especially, by the military genius of Napoleon. The acid test was that Britain was not defeated in the two darkest years of the wars – 1797 and 1805; in both years Pitt was in command. As friend and foe alike recognised at the end of January 1806, Pitt had bestridden a confusing and rapidly changing world with authority. He was not much loved but he was enormously respected. His legacy to the nineteenth century, if complex, was nevertheless formidable. An unheroic and pragmatic age might readily divest itself of over-sentimental notions about Pitt as the self-sacrificing pilot who weathered the biggest international storm which Britain had encountered since the fifteenth century. It is still left with a formidable leader who deserves to be remembered as one of the four greatest Prime Ministers in British history.

Further Reading

Biographies and other studies of Pitt

One biography produced in three volumes over the course of a generation, stands pre-eminent and will certainly remain the unchallenged work of reference and interpretation for the forseeable future. The broad chronological break points are 1788, 1797 and 1806:

J. Ehrman, *The Younger Pitt: Vol I The Years of Acclaim* (Constable, London, 1969)
——, *The Younger Pitt: Vol II The Reluctant Transition* (Constable, London, 1983)
——, *The Younger Pitt: Vol III The Consuming Struggle* (Constable, London, 1996)

Other valuable works include:
A. D. Harvey, *William Pitt the Younger, 1759–1806: A Bibliography* (Westport, Conn., 1989) is an admirably thorough listing of works about Pitt over almost two centuries
J. Holland Rose, *William Pitt and National Revival* (Bell, London, 1911)
——, *William Pitt and the Great War* (Bell, London, 1912) – both of these remain worth reading for their scholarship, though their interpretations are inevitably dated
J. Mori, 'William Pitt the Younger' in R. Eccleshall and G. Walker (eds), *Biographical Dictionary of British Prime Ministers* (Routledge, London, 1998a), pp. 85–94 – a valuable brief essay in introduction with a useful list of further reading
——, 'The Political Theory of William Pitt the Younger', *History* Vol. 83 (1998b), pp. 234–48
Earl Stanhope, *Life of the Right Honourable William Pitt* (4 vols, Murray, London, 1861) is also indispensable as a published work of reference since it includes extensive extracts from Pitt's correspondence

Biographies of other leading contemporary politicians

P. Jupp, *Lord Grenville* (Oxford University Press, 1985) – an excellent biography which also illuminates contemporary politics authoritatively

L. G. Mitchell, *Charles James Fox* (Oxford University Press, 1992) – erudite, elegant and shrewd

M. Peters, *The Elder Pitt* (Addison Wesley Longman, 1998) – a valuable new study of Pitt's father

P. Ziegler, *Addington* (Collins, London, 1965)

Textbooks and general assessments

J. Black (ed.), *British Politics and Society from Walpole to Pitt, 1742–89* (Macmillan, London, 1984) – rather less directly on Pitt than might be hoped but a useful chapter by Christie

I. Christie, *Wars and Revolutions, Britain 1760–1815* (Arnold, London, 1982)

E. J. Evans, *The Forging of the Modern State: Early Industrial Britain, 1783–1870* (2nd edn, Addison Wesley Longman, Harlow, 1996)

G. Holmes and D. Szechi, *The Age of Oligarchy: Pre-Industrial Britain, 1722–83* (Longman, London, 1993)

G. Newman, *The Rise of English Nationalism, 1740–1830* (Macmillan, London, 1997)

F. O'Gorman *The Long Eighteenth Century: British Political and Social History 1688–1832* (Arnold, London, 1997)

J. Steven Watson, *The Reign of George III* (Oxford University Press, Oxford, 1960)

Studies of the political system

J. Cannon, *Parliamentary Reform, 1640–1832* (Cambridge University Press, 2nd edn, Cambridge, 1980)

L. Colley, *Britons: Forging the Nation, 1707–1837* (Pimlico, London, 1994) – a brilliant, if overstated, account of the formation of national identity, with some very useful comments on the role, and image, of George III during the age of Pitt

J. Derry, *Politics in the Age of Fox, Pitt and Liverpool: Continuity and Transformation* (Macmillan, London, 1990)

H. T. Dickinson, *Liberty and Property: Political Ideology in Eighteenth-Century Britain* (Methuen, London, 1977)

A. D. Harvey, *Britain in the Early Nineteenth Century* (Batsford, London, 1978) – under-used by most students but a very effective guide to a complex shifting period in political allegiances

B. W. Hill, *British Parliamentary Parties, 1742–1832* (Allen & Unwin, London, 1985)

F. O'Gorman, *The Rise of Party in England* (Allen & Unwin, London, 1975)

——, *The Emergence of the British Two-Party System, 1760–1832* (Arnold, London, 1982)

J. J. Sack, *From Jacobite to Conservative: Reaction and Orthodoxy in Britain c.1760–1832* (Cambridge University Press, Cambridge, 1993) – cautions against regarding Pitt as a Tory

R. Thorne (ed.), *The History of Parliament: The House of Commons, 1790–1820* (History of Parliament Trust, London, 1986) – a mine of information about politicians and the political process

The impact of the French Revolution

H. Dickinson, *British Radicalism and the French Revolution, 1789–1815* (Blackwell, Oxford, 1985)

—— (ed.), *Britain and the French Revolution* (Macmillan, London, 1989)

C. Emsley, *British Society and the French Wars, 1793–1815* (Macmillan, London, 1979) – argues that Pitt's government exaggerated the threat from popular radicalism in the 1790s

——, 'Repression, "terror" and the rule of law in England during the decade of the French Revolution', *English Historical Review* 100 (1985), pp. 801–25

E. J. Evans, 'Englishness and Britishness: National Identities, c.1790–1870' in A. Grant and K. Stringer (eds), *Uniting the Kingdom?* (Routledge, London 1995), pp. 223–43

F. O'Gorman, *The Whig Party and the French Revolution* (Macmillan, London, 1967)

L. Mitchell, *Charles James Fox and the Disintegration of the Whig Party, 1782–1794* (Oxford University Press, Oxford, 1971)

J. Mori, *William Pitt and the French Revolution, 1785–95* (Keele/Edinburgh University Press, 1997) – a valuable modern study which suggests that Pitt was not much influenced ideologically by the French Revolution

E. P. Thompson, *The Making of the English Working Class* (Penguin, London, 1968) – classic, if controversial, account which is particularly rich on the political culture of working people as it developed in the 1790s

D. Wilkinson, 'The Pitt-Portland Coalition of 1794 and the Origins of the "Tory" party', *History* 83 (1998), pp. 249–64

Foreign policy and the wars with France

C. A. Bayly, *Imperial Meridian, 1780–1830* (Longman, London, 1989)

Jeremy Black, *A System of Ambition? British Foreign Policy, 1660–1793* (Longman, London, 1991)

——, *British Foreign Policy in an Age of Revolutions, 1783–93* (Cambridge University Press, Cambridge, 1994)

P. J. Cain and A. G. Hopkins, *British Imperialism: Innovation and Expansion, 1688–1914* (Longman, London, 1993)

M. Duffy, *Soldiers, Sugar & Seapower: The British Expeditions to the West Indies and the War against Revolutionary France* (Oxford University Press, Oxford, 1987)

Paul Kennedy, *The Rise and Fall of British Naval Mastery* (Allen Lane, London, 1976; 3rd edn, Fontana, London, 1991)

J. M. Sherwig, *Guineas and Gunpowder: British Foreign Aid in the Wars with France, 1793–1815* (Cambridge University Press, Cambridge, Mass., 1969)

Ireland

M. Elliott, 'Ireland and the French Revolution' in H. Dickinson (ed.), *Britain and the French Revolution* (Macmillan, London, 1989), pp. 83–101

R. F. Foster, *Modern Ireland, 1600–1972* (Penguin, London, 1988) – now the best one-volume history of Ireland

R. Kee, *The Green Flag, Vol. 1: The Most Distressful Country* (Quartet, London, 1976)

R. B. McDowell, *Ireland in the Age of Imperialism and Revolution, 1760–1801* (Clarendon, Oxford, 1991)